Exploring Feelings

Activities For Young Children

Susan B. Neuman, Ed.D.
and Renee P. Panoff

HUMANICS ™
LEARNING

P.O.Box 7400
Atlanta, Georgia 30357

Revised Printing 1994

Library of Congress Card Catalog Number: 82-81894
PRINTED IN THE UNITED STATES OF AMERICA
ISBN 0-89334-037-5

Book and Cover design by Laurie Svenkeson

To Sara, David, and Jesse

*who are just beginning to explore
their ever-enlarging world.*

Table of Contents

Fears   87

My World Around Me

The Community

The Environment   153

Living With Others   181

Understanding Children With Special Needs 213

Resources 221

INTRODUCTION

Children are naturally curious and eager to learn. Provided with a stimulating environment, they develop a sense of appreciation for and an understanding of themselves and the world around them by experimenting, touching, and interacting with others.

Perhaps the first and most important goal for children in these early years is the development of a positive self-image. Children who view themselves as important people feel more secure in exploring their environment, seeking independence and establishing social relationships.

One of the major objectives in preschool and kindergarten programs is the development of well-adjusted, cooperative people who are comfortable with themselves, their peers and the adults with whom they interact. EXPLORING FEELINGS has been written for the teacher, paraprofessional, student, parent or anyone else who is responsible for providing and coordinating educational activities that will help preschool children develop self-confidence, independence and creative freedom. The book contains many ideas that can be used in a group or home setting. Experiences with everyday ideas and materials help children understand and appreciate their world.

The major emphasis in these activities is affective. These activities utilize teaching methods which actively involve the whole child in the learning process as he or she searches for information, cooperates with others and makes decisions. Music, art, and self-expression are interwoven in the activities to encourage children's interest and involvement in the learning environment.

Imaginative play serves an important role in helping children understand their feelings and their world. When assuming a role in creative play, children are in a sense working through who and what they are. When children take on roles (firefighter, school teacher, etc.) they are developing an awareness of the functions provided by the different people they see around them. Children playing "school" will find that school seems less frightening or alien to them. Few restrictions are placed on reality by children's imaginations. Such play encourages original thinking and an understanding of the more subtle aspects of adult communication.

Many children have the basic ability for imaginative play, but need some form of encouragement from a trusted adult. The adult can assist by facilitating and observing play, but he or she should avoid becoming overly involved once the play has begun. Dramatic play can also be enhanced by including open-ended, flexible materials (paint, sand, building blocks) which lend themselves to long-term imaginative uses. An interesting, inviting environment which creates a climate for fostering self-concepts, social responsibility and cooperation is most important for developing imaginative play, self-expression and human growth.

The ideas described in this book are designed to enhance the social, emotional, moral and creative development of children in the early childhood setting. In some cases, these activities might already be part of the children's imaginative play repetoire, such as creative "hospital" play. Parents and teachers are encouraged to use this play, however, as a vehicle for helping children recognize and verbalize feelings about given situations. To a large extent a child can overcome fears of separation, night time, or visits to the doctor or dentist, for example, when we help make the unknown become more familiar.

1

Helping children develop a healthy personality, a positive self-image, social responsibility, creativity and a sense of morality is a major responsibility for those working in the early childhood setting. The quality of children's lives depends upon how well we fulfill this responsibility.

All About Me

Infants first begin to explore their environment by exploring their own bodies. At this stage they are attempting to understand where they end and the rest of the world begins. Their attitudes toward their bodies summarize their interactions with themselves and their world. A child's awareness of his or her physical body is important in the development of self-concept as well as a sense of physical coordination.

One way a child develops an awareness of his or her body is by exploring body parts. Children learn that different parts of the body function in different ways. They learn about the capabilities of their bodies through firsthand experiences.

During these early years it is most important for adults to help children acquire positive self-images and to help them learn to move their bodies skillfully and use their abilities successfully. When children develop an appreciation of themselves, they will begin to feel more secure in exploring their environment, seeking independence and developing social relationships.

Shadow Play

Purpose:

- To help the children learn how a shadow is formed
- To help the children develop imaginative use of their bodies as they form "shadows" with a friend
- To encourage cooperative play as two children work together to form "shadows" with their bodies
- To help children understand the difference between light and dark
- To help children feel comfortable with the dark

Materials:

- Flashlight
- Large sheet of white paper

Activity:

Form a shadow by shining a flashlight onto the large sheet of paper. Invite the children to move their hands between the light and the paper. Ask them, "What are these designs called?"

Encourage the children to make hand movements which result in fun shadows.

Discuss how the shadow is a copycat! The shadow does everything the hand does! It makes pictures with light and dark.

Tell the children, "We're going to play 'The Shadow Game'."

Pair two children together and ask them to stand face to face. Ask one child in each pair to be the other child's shadow. Tell them that means any motion the first child makes has to be copied by the second child.

Encourage the "leader" to make all kinds of movements and let the "shadow" follow closely. You might suggest: jumping, reaching, waving, rocking, etc.

To heighten the imagination, you might ask, "What kinds of ways can you move your head, arms, legs, and other parts of your body?"

After a period of time, ask the children to change places, letting the former "shadow" become the leader, and vice versa.

5

Body Awareness Through Rhythm

Purpose:

- To further children's awareness of their bodies
- To encourage children to develop their listening skills
- To help children feel good about their bodies

Materials:

- Beanbags OR
- String
- Old socks and
- Beans

Activity:

Make bean bags with the children by partially filling large socks with beans and tying them tightly with string. OR distribute commercially manufactured bean bags among the children.

Tell the children they will play a dancing game. They will need to use their ears to listen and to follow directions. When you call out to do something with the bean bag, the children are to do as you say.

Play some music and begin. You can direct the children to do a variety of body movements. The following are a few examples:
- Put the bean bag on your head (or any other body part)
- Hold the bean bag over your head and skip
- Tiptoe and try not to wake up the beans in the bag

My Body Has Different Parts

Purpose:

● To help children learn the various parts of their body and how these parts are put together

Materials:

● Pictures of people

Activity:

To help the children become more aware of various parts of their bodies, play "Simon Says". Then, show them pictures of people with various parts of their bodies missing. Encourage them to name the missing parts. You could use magazine pictures, draw your own, or use other variations.

Sounds Within Me

Purpose:

- To help children gain an understanding of the inner workings of their bodies

Materials:

- Stethoscope

Activity:

Invite the children to use the stethoscope to listen to various parts of their body. The following are examples:
- Placing the stethoscope on the cheek and making different sounds with the tongue, lips and teeth.
- Listening to the throat as they swallow.
- Listening to the stomach area as liquid is swallowed.
- Listening to the heart and pressure points such as the wrist or neck.
- Listening to their scalps as they scratch their heads.
- Listening to their wrists as they bend their hand back and forth.
- Listening to their pulse.

Our Bodies Are All Different

Purpose:

- To encourage children to feel comfortable with their own individuality

Materials:

- None

Activity:

Invite the children to take off one of their shoes. Have them feel inside their shoe and note the small indentations formed by parts of their feet. Talk about how each foot is different and makes its own special markings. Have the children put one of their shoes in a pile and invite them to try on each others' shoes. Talk about how funny they feel and note that none feels as comfy as their own. Encourage them to see that each foot is built a little differently because each person is put together a little differently.

Body Dolls

Purpose:

- To create dolls for imaginative play that are likenesses of themselves

Materials:

- Large sheets of paper (butcher paper)
- Stapler
- Paints

Activity:

One at a time, have each child lie on top of a double thickness of large paper. Trace the child's outline and cut the body shape from both sheets of paper. Using a mirror, talk to the children about their physical features and encourage them to paint their likeness on the doll figure. Have the children paint their fronts on one cutout and their backs on the other. When dry, staple the two doll cutouts together around the edges. Leave an opening so that you can stuff the figure with newspaper, then finish stapling. The children can then use these doll figures in dramatic play in the classroom or at home.

Body Jobs

Purpose:

- To help children understand how parts of their bodies work for them
- To help children see that they are in control of their bodies

Materials:

- None

Activity:

Describe jobs performed by various parts of the body and have the children guess which body part is being described. Some examples of these "body riddles" could be:

- "What keeps your head cool in the summer and warm in the winter?" (hair)
- "What helps keep perspiration from dripping into your eyes?" (eyebrows)
- "What helps you run to first base?" (legs)
- "What helps you balance on the end of your feet?" (toes)
- "What helps you hold a fork to eat?" (fingers)
- "What helps you smell cookies baking?" (nose)
- "What helps you hear the telephone ring?" (ears)

Then invite the children to pose some further body riddles. End the game by noting,
"Our body is like a machine that is made up of many, many parts that work for us. We are lucky to have such wonderful equipment that makes work and play so exciting!"

Who Am I?

Purpose:

- To help children understand that costumes and disguises can change their appearance but not change who they are

Materials:

- Paper bags
- Scissors
- Paint
- Glue
- Yarn

Activity:

Discuss with the children about ways we change our appearance. Examples might be when someone gets a new haircut or shaves off a mustache, or when someone removes his or her glasses or wears sunglasses. Ask them if it sometimes feels strange or even a bit scary to see someone we know look different than he/she did before. Note that it feels comfortable when we realize that the person is really the same even though he/she seemed so new and different at first.

Tell the children, "We're going to have some fun changing the way we look." Make paper bag masks. Cut out spaces for the eyes and nose. Invite the children to paint the masks and glue yarn for hair.

When completed and dry, let the children play with the masks. They may examine their appearances in a mirror and try to guess who is behind each mask. Note that even though the masks make us look different, we're really the same people as before.

The Book About Me

Purpose:

- To help children gain a fuller awareness of themselves as individuals
- To help children feel important and special

Materials:

- Construction paper
- Ribbon
- Crayons

Activity:

Tell the children that each of us is an important, special person. Invite them to create a book that tells much about who they are. To make the book, tie several sheets of paper together with three pieces of ribbon. On the first page, print the title, "The Book About Me," and have the children draw a picture of themselves underneath. The succeeding pages can include various aspects of the children's lives. Print a caption on each page and let the children illustrate it. You might include:

- "Draw a picture of your family."
- "Draw a picture of your best friend."
- "Draw a picture of your house."
- "Where were you born?"
- "What is your favorite color?" "Food?" "Drink?"
- "What time of day do you like best?"
- "What is your favorite day of the week?"
- "What are your favorite clothes?"
- "Do you have a pet?"
- "I am sad when _____."
- "I am happy when _____."

You could share these books by reading them to the group at story time. How important and special to hear teacher read a complete book about you in the story time setting!

Growing Up - Up - Up

Purpose:

- To help children feel proud of their achievements
- To help children view their growth as a continuous process from birth onward

Materials:

- Music

Activity:

Ask the children, "What could you do when you were a baby?"

After some discussion, put on some music and encourage the children to act out the behavioral examples the group came up with, using creative movement.

Then ask the group, "What kinds of things can you do *now* that you could not do as babies?"

Again, invite the children to express these ideas physically to music.

Freeze!

Purpose:

- To practice body control
- To encourage children to feel comfortable about moving their bodies freely
- To develop the ability to listen

Materials:

- Music

Activity:

Play music and encourage the children to move freely. Tell them that when they hear the music stop they must stop their bodies in mid-action and "freeze". Then when the music begins again they may again move creatively.

Puppet Play: Feeling Your Body At Work And Working With Another Body

Purpose:

- To come to a greater awareness of how our bodies move
- To heighten imagination through body awareness
- To encourage cooperative play through physical communication

Materials:

- Colored yarn
- Chairs

Activity:

In pairs, let the children pretend to be puppets and puppeteers. One child is a puppet, with long strands of yarn tied to his/her arms and legs. The other child, the puppeteer, stands on a chair and holds the ends of the yarn. Let the children make up situations to act out as they begin to play together as puppet and puppeteer.

I Can Do This Well

Purpose:

- To bolster the children's self-images and to help them feel confident in their abilities
- To encourage children to see that each person is capable of doing different things at different levels of competence

Materials:

- None

Activity:

Sit in a circle and ask the children to tell about something that they can do well. The children might like to show the others how well they can perform a particular task. Some examples could be skipping, hopping, dancing, singing, throwing a ball, putting on a coat, tying shoe laces, riding a tricycle, climbing, etc. Further, the children could be invited to bring something from home that would help show a certain expertise.

Discuss with the children how wonderful it is that we're all so different. It's very interesting to see that what is easy for one is difficult for another. But the important thing is that *each* of us is able to do *some* things very well, and that makes us all such special people.

I Like Me

Purpose:

- To promote feelings of self-worth

Materials:

- None

Activity:

In a group, each person mentions some things he likes about himself. Then, using a mirror, each child tells him/herself, "I like me because _____."
If the children need a little encouragement, you might help by asking a pointed question or making a statement such as:

- "How do you help your mom at home?"
- "Can you share some toys with friends?"
- "I saw you help Judy put away the blocks. That was a lovely thing to do."

In this way, everyone will share good feelings about him/herself as well as his/her class-mates.

Proud To Be Me

Purpose:

- To become more aware of how each of us is put together
- To develop positive feelings about one's body

Materials:

- Large sheet of paper (perhaps brown wrapping paper or butcher paper)
- Paint
- Pencil
- Mirror

Activity:

Each child lies on top of a large sheet of paper, face up and with arms and legs separated. Using a pencil, outline the child's body. Cut out the form.

Invite the children to paint their features, clothes, etc., on these cutouts. Children can use a mirror to get a sense of their facial parts and hair before actually painting. After completion, it's fun to tack these figures on the wall and get a full view of ourselves. This is an excellent activity to do at the beginning of the year, or for Parents Night, when everyone is still unfamiliar with the others in the classroom.

Healthy Snacking

Purpose:

- To help encourage positive feelings about healthy snacking
- To help children learn to control their pre-dinner snacking independently

Materials:

- Magazines
- Glue
- Construction paper

Activity:

Discuss with the children that it is important to be careful about what and when we eat in order to care for our bodies. You might note that eating before dinner makes us not hungry for the big meal and that too many sugary foods are not good for our teeth.

Talk about the foods you might consider healthy snacks. They might include raw vegetables, fruits, juices, nuts, raisins and cheese. Let the children look through magazines, cutting up pictures and gluing them onto a piece of construction paper as a collage. You can send these collages home to the parents with a suggestion that they be put on the refrigerator at the child's eye level. The collage might remind the child of the snacks permissible at certain times—particularly when dinner time approaches.

Foods I Like

Purpose:

- To help children view themselves as discerning people with tastes unique to themselves
- To help children feel positive about the food they eat

Materials:

- 5" x 7" file cards
- Shoe box
- Rubber bands
- Glue

Activity:

Discuss with the children their special food preferences. Have them clip pictures of foods they like from magazines, newspapers, old recipe books and such. Then have them glue each picture separately onto a 5" x 7" file card. The children can group these cards into breakfast, lunch, and dinner foods. As children begin to experiment with new foods, they might add to their card file. The cards may be sent home to help parents prepare favorite foods for their children. In addition, these cards may be used for dramatic play as the children plan "meals" for each other or their dolls. Using them in a play situation might encourage some children to "try" new foods in a nonthreatening situation.

Silhouettes

Purpose:

● To give children an opportunity to view and relate to images of themselves

Materials:

● Flashlight
● White paper

Activity:

Talk about how light forms shadows or pictures of our bodies. Shine a light on the side of a child's head causing the head to form a shadow. On a blank sheet of paper pinned to the wall, trace the outline of the shadow.

You may choose to cut out the silhouettes and have the child paste them on black paper for a special present to take home to Mom or Dad from school.

Bending And Moving

Purpose:

• To help children understand how our joints work

Materials:

• Cardboard
• Paper fasteners

Activity:

Encourage the children to feel their arms, wrists, legs, knees and ankles move. Note that these spots allow us to twist our arms and legs and are called joints.

Invite the children to make cutouts of people that have movable joints. Ask the children to draw, color and cut out a person-figure from cardboard or poster board. (You cut it out if it is too difficult for the children.) Cut places for the wrists, elbows, shoulders, hips, knees and ankles. Overlap the cut edges and fasten the pieces with brass colored paper fasteners. The children will have little models which they can use to explore freely how their joints move. Help the children name the various joints.

As a game, you could ask the children to place the doll in a funny position and then see if they can imitate the paper figure. They will then see not only how their bodies bend, but also how their joints' movement is limited.

My Hands Have Jobs

Purpose:

- To help children understand how our arms and hands function
- To help children appreciate how our arms and hands work for us

Materials:

- Pictures of animals

Activity:

Talk with the children about some of the many things our arms and hands can do. Make note of the different parts of the hands and arms as the children demonstrate how their arms and hands work. For instance, they could use a fork or spoon, paint with a brush, color with crayons, model clay, clap, wave or bring food to the mouth.

Then show pictures of different animals and ask, "Which of these animals do not have hands or arms?"

After this discussion, play the game "Give Me A Hand." One person stands and clasps his hands behind his back. Another person stands in back of this person, slips his arms through the front person's arms and pretends that his arms belong to the person in front. Playing this way, the children can try together some of the various tasks listed before or look in the mirror for a funny feeling.

Footprints

Purpose:

- To help the children feel proud of their bodies

Materials:

- White paper
- Water-based paints

Activity:

Have the children closely examine the soles of their feet. Encourage them to look for lines, bumps, and different textures.

Have each child step in some water-based paint and then step on a sheet of paper. Print the child's name at the top of the paper. Talk about how the footprint appears. Note how each person's feet are unique and different.

Shoe Rubbings

Purpose:

- To experience the beauty and individuality of textures
- To encourage children to think positively about their own individuality

Materials:

- Paper
- Crayons

Activity:

Have the children explore the soles of their shoes. Talk about how they look and feel.

Place a sheet of paper over the sole and rub with a crayon. Talk about how the designs differ from one shoe to another. Explain that each one is different and special as each one of us is different and yet very special.

Hand And Feet Prints

Purpose:

- To help children appreciate the uniqueness and beauty of their own bodies

Materials:

- Plaster of paris

Activity:

Have the children take off their shoes and socks. Prepare some plaster of paris and form the material into small slabs. Invite the children to gently press their hands and feet into the plaster. When dry, the plaster of paris forms a permanent record of their feet and hands.

When the casts are dry, let the children gently try to fit their hands and feet into each other's prints. Talk about how each one is different and that no hand or foot fits into our prints as well as our own.

Our Fingerprints Are Special

Purpose:

- To help children see that their fingerprints are unique

Materials:

- Paint
- Paper
- Magnifying glass

Activity:

Talk about how each of us is different — right down to our fingerprints! Have the children look closely at and feel the tips of their thumbs. Talk about the lines they find on the tips of their thumbs and have them examine each others' thumbs. Use a magnifying glass if possible. Note that the line design on each person's thumb is different.

Invite the children to use their thumbs to make prints by dipping their thumbs in paint and pressing them gently onto paper. Try to look for the designs made by the lines of the fingers.

Note that, just as each person's thumbs are different, so, too, is each person's picture. That's because each of us is different and special.

Growth Chart

Purpose:

● To help children view their individual growth in a concrete way

Materials:

● Tape in various colors

Activity:

As each child stands against a wall, mark his/her height. Then tape a strip of tape on the wall from the floor up to the mark. Label each tape with the child's name. Periodically remeasure each child and add the appropriate amount of tape. By changing the color of the tape each time you measure, you'll help the children gain a clearer and more concrete view of how much they have grown.

For children a bit older, have a yardstick available and explain how to measure and read it. The children can use the stick to measure the taped heights.

Taking Care Of Our Bodies

Purpose:

● To help children develop good health habits including proper toothbrushing, exercise, washing, eating, and sleeping, through imaginative play

Materials:

● Flannel Board
● Cut-out pictures of a:
      Toothbrush
      Comb
      Wash cloth
      Dinner plate of food
      Person running
      Person sleeping
      Scissors

Activity:

A. Ask the children how we can take care of our bodies and keep them healthy and strong.
Put representational pictures on the flannel board. You may encourage the children by asking prompting questions such as:

● "What do we do when our nails get too long and become scratchy?" (Scissors)
● "What do we do when our hair becomes so long it falls in our eyes?" (Scissors, haircut)
● "How else do we take care of our hair?" "How do we keep it clean, neat?" (Wash, comb)
● "What do we do when our bodies feel tired and sleepy?" (Sleep, rest)
● "In what ways do we make our bodies strong?" (Exercise, good food)
● "How do we keep our bodies clean?" (Bath)
● "How do we take care of our teeth?" (Toothbrush)

B.   Ask the children to lie down on the floor and to pretend they are fast asleep in their beds. Then wake them up with a, "Good morning! Let's stretch and push all the sleepiness away."

Tell the children it's morning and we want to start taking care of our body. Ask them what kinds of things they would do during the day to keep it healthy and to keep it strong. You might include the situations and examples discussed in Activity A, as well as any you and the children might think of. Be sure to practice proper toothbrushing (up and down) and discuss how we can avoid cavities by eating fewer sweets.

End the game by telling the children, "It's nighttime. The stars are out and the sun is down. It's time for us to go to sleep. It's time for us to give our bodies a rest. Let's brush our teeth one more time before we go to sleep."

Tell the children to lie down to "pretend" to go to sleep and you will come around and "tuck them in."

Feelings

Young children are just beginning to develop an awareness of their own emotions and feelings. A significant part of the early childhood curriculum involves helping children deal with these emotions in positive ways.

The activities in the beginning of this section focus on a variety of feelings: happiness, sadness, frustration, anger, etc. These ideas attempt to introduce children to a myriad of emotions, emphasizing that all people experience these feelings at times. These activities also include experiences which give children a chance to explore feelings through their senses.

Feeling happy and expressing love is another theme presented in this section. Children are encouraged to explore the many ways of showing we care for other people as well as ourselves. These activities are followed by an emphasis on angry feelings. The ideas presented here are most effectively used during a group lesson rather than during a time of conflict between individual children. The objective is not to resolve specific conflicts but to encourage children to understand their angry feelings and to express them in nonviolent ways.

Finally, there is a special section which focuses on common fears. Even the youngest of children experience instances of emotional stress. A trusted adult can help them work through these negative emotions by gaining familiarity with the anxiety-producing situation or through role-playing. When children feel free to express their emotions, their feelings of self-confidence, leading to further personal growth, can flourish.

Different Feelings

Purpose:

- To help children see that people express many different feelings

Materials:

- Magazines
- Travel brochures
- Advertising booklets
- Glue
- Construction paper

Activity:

Talk with the children about how we all have many feelings. Sometimes we are happy, sad, surprised, angry, impatient, etc. Ask them to give some examples of when they have felt these and other feelings. Clip out pictures in magazines, brochures, advertising booklets, etc., of people expressing various feelings. Then let the children glue them on colored construction paper to make collages of "People and Feelings."

Colors Are Feelings

Purpose:

● To encourage children to associate colors with feelings

Materials:

● Colored construction paper

Activity:

Tell the children that colors can make us think of many things—things that make us happy, sad, funny, or feel one of many other different feelings.

Have ready an assortment of colored construction paper. Holding up one at a time, ask the children, "What does this color remind you of?" or "What does this color make you feel?"

Encourage the children to name the color and relate to it in a personal way. Some examples might be:

● "Brown reminds me of hot chocolate on a cold wintry day."
● "Green reminds me of the first day of Spring."

These special remembrances can be written down and collected in a special "Color Book" for those rainy, "gray" days.

Simon Says It With Feeling

Purpose:

- To help children relate to and express warm feelings

Materials:

- None

Activity:

Play Simon Says, but instead of touching body parts, have the children show various emotions. Some examples are:

- "Simon Says, 'Show that you are surprised to see a present on your bed!'"

- "Simon Says, 'Show that you are mad because your dog ate your book!'"

- "Simon Says, 'Show that you're sleepy.'"

What Is This Person Feeling?

Purpose:

- To develop an understanding of people's feelings through observation
- To foster empathic responses in young children

Materials:

- Photographs or magazines

Activity:

Show the children pictures of people involved in various situations in which they express diverse emotions, such as fear, anger, or disappointment. Magazines, photographs, newspapers and books are all good sources of such pictures.

Ask the children,
- "What do you think is happening here?"
- "How are these people feeling?"
- "How do you know?"
- "When have *you* felt this way?"

Encourage the children to discuss various situations which bring out particular feelings: holiday excitement and later disappointment, fear of coming to school for the first time, staying over at a friend's house, etc. These discussions may help children realize that many people share the same type of feelings.

Sorting Out Feelings

Purpose:

- To recognize facial expressions as reflective of feelings
- To discriminate different feelings and expressions
- To recognize feelings and verbally express them

Materials:

- Cardboard
- Crayon or marker
- Scissors

Activity:

Draw 5 identical happy faces, 5 sad faces, 5 surprised faces and 5 angry faces (20 faces in all). Show one of each to the children. Have them tell you the feeling it indicates. Play the "Sorting Out Feelings Game." Ask the child to turn a card over, imitate the facial expression, and express the feeling pictured in an individual way. As you and the children finish with the cards, put them into categories: "Happy", "Sad", "Surprised", "Angry".

Guess The Feeling

Purpose:

- To recognize various feelings by one's facial expressions
- To see that everyone experiences a myriad of emotional reactions

Materials:

- None

Activity:

A person's face often shows many feelings. Demonstrate a variety of facial expressions and let the children try to guess the emotion you are conveying. Then let the children take turns expressing their feelings with facial expressions. Each time they do so, ask them when they have experienced that particular feeling before.

Some feelings to explore are:

- happy
- sad
- wounded
- thrilled
- queazy
- confused
- furious

Communicating Feelings Without Words

Purpose:

- To help children get in touch with their bodies as communicators of feelings

Materials:

- Music

Activity:

Discuss with the children ways their bodies communicate, or tell, how they feel. Some examples could be:

- Tapping feet say "I'm in a hurry"
- Scolding fingers say "I'm angry"
- Hands grabbing a doll say "I want this"
- A hug says "I like you and I want to be close to you"
- Shrugging shoulders say "I don't know"
- A wrinkled up nose says "I don't understand"
- Chattering teeth say "I am freezing!"

Then, play some music and encourage the children to use creative movement to express these and other feelings.

Mirror Play

Purpose:

- To encourage children to draw from within themselves various emotions and then to be able to express them visually

Materials:

- Mirror

Activity:

Pass the mirror from child to child and invite the children to show on their face a particular emotion. Some examples could be:

- disgust
- sadness
- joy
- thirsty
- frustrated
- impatient
- annoyed
- furious
- cranky
- silly

Ask each child if he/she can think of a situation in which he/she felt the emotion conveyed.

As a further activity, you might ask the children to role-play the situation which caused the particular emotion.

Mirror, Mirror

Purpose:

- To encourage children to recognize feelings in others
- To help foster empathetic relationships

Materials:

- None

Activity:

Place the children in pairs. Tell them that one child in each pair will pretend to be the other's mirror. As one child shows an emotion, the partner should reflect his/her expression. After several feelings have been explored, have the children in each pair trade roles.

If children have difficulty in demonstrating various emotions, try giving them a key statement, such as:

- "You are opening up your presents for your birthday."
- "You are visiting the doctor and you have been waiting for 1 hour."

Sounds That Tell Feelings

Purpose:

● To help encourage children to look for clues in their environment that tell them how others might be feeling

Materials:

● Tape recorder
● Tape with special sounds

Activity:

Tape-record sounds of people and animals. Play the tape to the children and have them identify the sounds. Discuss how the person/animal might be feeling when he makes the sound heard.

Some examples might be:

● purring cat
● barking dog
● chattering bird
● honking geese
● galloping horse
● crying baby
● laughter
● a person saying "sh-h-h"
● whistling
● humming
● snoring
● sound of skipping feet
● applause

Understanding these sounds can help children be aware of how other animals/people are feeling.

Fingerpaint Feelings

Purpose:

- To express various emotions through the experience of fingerpaints

Materials:

- Fingerpaint
- Shiny fingerpaint paper or plastic table top

Activity:

Encourage the children to explore and express a variety of feelings using their hands and fingerpaint. Ask the children to show how they feel when the following types of experiences might happen:

- Someone knocks over your building
- You drop your ice cream cone
- You find someone's lost puppy for him
- You go to the cookie jar and it is empty
- A friend shares her dessert with you
- You get to go to the circus
- Someone quietly creeps behind you and yells "BOO!"

The children can think of many more personal experiences to express with paint. The children will use the same paper to go from expressing one feeling to another. Remember, the experience and process are what matters in this activity, not the end product.

The finger paint may be purchased in stores, or made from the following recipe:
   2 tablespoons Vano Starch
   1 teaspoon colored tempera

Giving Of Yourself

Purpose:

- To encourage children to exchange and share with one another

Materials:

- Bread
- Sandwich fillers
- Plastic knives

Activity:

Spread out an array of bread and sandwich fillers, such as peanut butter, sliced eggs, jelly, cream cheese, tuna fish, and bologna for the children. Invite them to each make a sandwich. Then ask each child to cut his/her sandwich into quarters, keeping one quarter and passing three on to three other people. In this way, each child shares his/her sandwich with three other people.

You could say, "This is a fine way to share and give of yourselves. Each of us has made a sandwich, and three of our friends can enjoy it with us!"

I Like Today

Purpose:

- To help teach the days of the week in a concrete way
- To help children get in touch with how they spend time
- To help children see the richness of their lives

Materials:

- Colored paper or cardboard

Activity:

Take a large sheet of paper or cardboard. Make seven columns and label each column consecutively with the days of the week. Discuss with the children what happens on each day. Write these activities or occurrences in the appropriate column. Let the children illustrate the columns with pictures of the activities named. Some examples could be:

- dancing school
- gymnastics
- religious school
- stay with babysitter
- go to school
- go to church or synagogue
- Mom or Dad home from work
- get to stay up later
- go shopping
- birthday party

Children can use this beginning calendar to help schedule events and organize their days.

Cookie Feelings

Purpose:

- To help children see that faces can show how we feel

Materials:

- Cookie dough
- Oven

Activity:

Talk about ways our faces show how we feel. Demonstrate some ways and encourage the children to do so too, looking in a mirror.

Then, using homemade cookie dough or refrigerator cookie dough that the children slice and roll out, make faces with icing that depict various feelings. Bake the cookies.

After a discussion of the variety of feelings, let the children choose their favorite and enjoy.

Make A Face

Purpose:

- To develop an awareness of facial features
- To enjoy making funny faces

Materials:

- Magazines, construction paper
- Glue
- Scissors

Activity:

Talk with the children about the various parts of the face and the jobs these facial parts do. For instance, the nose smells for us. Sometimes it smells yummy things like baking cookies, and other times it smells unpleasant things like rotten eggs.

Invite the children to clip pictures of facial features from magazines. Then encourage them to glue these features on construction paper in collages of funny faces.

It's Fun To Feel Textures

Purpose:

- To enjoy feeling and discriminating textures

Materials:

- Heavy posterboard or wood
- Swatches of material
- Glue

Activity:

Glue swatches of material with diverse textures to a large sheet of heavy poster board or wood.

Discuss with the children how different textures feel to the touch. "Texture" is a word that refers to the way things feel. Display the Texture Board and encourage the children to explore the textures and talk about the way they feel—soft, rough, coarse, slippery, furry, wiry, crunchy, sticky, smooth, velvety, wet, dry, sharp, dull or spongy. Start with simple objects and add to the board as time goes on.

Textures In My Life

Purpose:

● To encourage children to relate to textures in a personal, experiential way

Materials:

● Texture Board

Activity:

Invite the children to feel the textures on the Texture Board that you have made. Have them close their eyes. As they do so, ask them: "When you feel this, what do you think about?" "What does the texture remind you of?"

The children will begin to relate to textures by associating them with important events, people, or experiences in their lives.

Imagining How Things Feel

Purpose:

- To encourage children to relate physically to textures in their environment

Materials:

- None

Activity:

Invite the children to use creative body movement to convey textures. First, ask them to think of things or places they know about and describe how they feel to the touch. Then ask them to use creative body movements to act out the sensation of these textures.

Some examples might be:

- ice cream melting on a plate
- stamping through dry autumn leaves
- walking barefoot on hot sand
- chewing a wad of bubble gum
- peeling a burst bubble off your face
- petting a soft kitten
- kissing Dad before he shaves
- pulling a melted marshmallow off a stick

Smells I Like And Smells I Don't Like

Purpose:

- To help children develop their sense of smell
- To help children become aware of how they feel about different smells in their experience

Materials:

- Plastic containers
- Substances to sniff

Activity:

Collect small plastic containers. Clean, empty spice or pill jars work well. In each one, place an item or substance with a distinctive smell. Have the children smell each one and talk about what the substance is.

Then, have the children close their eyes and guess each substance by only smelling it. Afterwards, invite the children to group the smells according to whether or not they find them enjoyable.

Some substances to try might be:

- garlic
- ginger
- cinnamon
- peanuts
- perfume
- onion

- yeast and water
- lemon peel
- cloves
- sea shells
- peppermint
- maple syrup

Relating To Smells

Purpose:

● To encourage children to associate smells with personal experiences

Materials:

● Containers from the previous lesson

Activity:

Using the containers filled with various substances you prepared for the previous lesson, encourage the children to sniff and describe what the smell makes them think of. Have them close their eyes and describe a scene that the particular smell reminds them of.

Trying New Things

Purpose:

- To develop self-confidence by trying something new
- To encourage children to try new tasks and tastes

Materials:

- An unusual assortment of fruits and vegetables, such as
  kiwi
  avocado
  mango
  papaya
  pomegranate
  squash

- Paper plates
- Plastic knives and spoons
- Napkins
- Garbage bag

Activity:

We learn new things by trying them.

Show the children the vegetables and fruits and discuss the names. Tell the children, "These are probably new fruits and vegetables to us. Let's get to know these fruits and vegetables."

Encourage the children to explore the fruits and vegetables by touching, lifting, feeling, smelling. Ask the children to sort them according to size, color, shape and category (fruit or vegetable). Say, "How can we really get to know these foods?" "Let's try them. Let's have a tasting party!"

To the extent feasible, have the children cut open the food. Then, everybody has a fun time learning to taste new foods!

NOTE: The emphasis in this activity is on *trying* new foods rather than on eating and finishing them.

Is It Sour? Is It Sweet?

Purpose:

● To help children differentiate taste sensations

Materials:

● Examples of foods that are sour or sweet

Activity:

First invite the children to taste a bit of sugar and note that we call this taste "sweet". Then give them a touch of lemon and note that we call this flavor "sour".

Then arrange an array of taste sensations that are either sour or sweet. Some taste sensations might be:

● maple syrup
● apple
● honey
● lime
● grapefruit
● grapefruit juice
● uncooked jello

As the children taste each one, have them note whether it is sweet or sour in taste. Ask the children to describe what sweet and sour tastes feel like in their mouths.

Taste Transformations

Purpose:

- To alert children to how foods and tastes are transferred through various processes in our environment

Materials:

- Foods used in various food preparation experiences

Activity:

As an ongoing activity in your curriculum, each time you cook with the children, encourage them to taste the ingredients before mixing, blending, or cooking. During and after completion of the cooking process, have the children try to detect the individual tastes of the ingredients as the blending or heating transforms their consistency and state. Make special note when you add spices, particularly sugar and salt. Further, encourage the children to talk about how they feel when the food changes state. For instance, some children love to taste the crispy vegetables as they cut them up for soup, but find the cooked vegetables unappealing.

Some good choices for cooking and food preparation experiences are:

- ice cream
- applesauce
- cakes, cookies
- fruit pies
- hamburger
- mashed potatoes
- chocolate milk
- milkshake
- soup

Feeling Box

Purpose:

- To help children relate to the physical world around them in a tactile manner

Materials:

- Bag
- Common objects

Activity:

Out of sight of the children, place several objects in a bag. Use common objects from the classroom or the home. Invite the children to feel the objects in the bag, without looking inside. Have them describe what an object feels like, how it makes them feel, and then have them try to guess what it is.

A variation of this activity is to create a smelling box. Put an interesting kind of food in the box such as peanuts, and let the children guess what the smell is.

Touching Shelf

Purpose:

- To encourage children to explore objects through touch

Materials:

- Objects of tactile interest common to the experiences of the children

Activity:

Set aside a shelf on which to have accessible objects which the children may freely explore through touch. These objects should be ones common to the experiences of the children and perhaps tied in with the curriculum. For instance, if you take a walk along the seashore and look for signs of the sea, collect sand and shells and display them on the "Touching Shelf" Periodically change and add to the shelf as the interests of the children develop.

Some fun things to explore tactilly are:

- feathers
- stones
- pebbles
- bottle caps
- corks
- marbles
- pine cones
- acorns
- textile materials

Experiencing Music

Purpose:

- To encourage children to feel comfortable with their bodies as they enjoy making and responding to music

Materials:

- Paper
- Oatmeal box
- Shoe box
- Rubber bands
- Paper plates
- Buttons or beans
- Stapler
- Tape
- Household items such as wooden spoons and pot lids

Activity:

Put on some music. First, have the children listen with their eyes closed. Then invite them to move freely. Ask the children how they feel when they move to music.

Have materials ready for the children to make homemade instruments.

- A decorated oatmeal box becomes a drum.
- Heavy rubber bands wrapped around a shoebox make a funny guitar.
- Colored paper folded like a funnel or cone and decorated with streamers can be a horn.
- 2 lids are much like a pair of cymbals.
- 2 decorated paper plates filled with several buttons or beans and stapled together make fine marracas.

Put on some marching music and encourage the children to parade, playing their instruments, with joyful abandon.

You could later introduce the children to the concepts "soft" and "loud" and help them learn to control their movements. First demonstrate soft and loud music. Then play the marching music and invite the children to parade and play their instruments. You could then discuss how our bodies can still feel free and joyous even though we at times control how we move.

Sinking And Floating

Purpose:

- To understand the concept of sinking and floating
- To experience how sinking and floating might feel

Materials:

- Basin or tub of water
- An assortment of objects which might float or sink
- Music

Activity:

Ask the children if they can tell you what "float" and "sink" mean. Using a tub of water and small objects, demonstrate that when an object rests on the top or surface of the water, we say it floats; when an object falls to the bottom, we say it sinks. Offer the children a variety of common objects with which to experiment. Some might be: a cork, crayon, paper clip, paper boat, empty pill container, spoon, coin, straw, tongue depressor, Q-tip, rubber band.

Then, let the children pretend to be some of these common objects. If desired, play music to accompany their creative movement as the children pretend to sink and float.

Listen For The Sound

Purpose:

- To encourage children to listen carefully and discriminate sounds

Materials:

- Orange juice cans
- Various substances and small objects to shake
- Tape

Activity:

Place various substances that can be shaken easily into clean, empty orange juice cans. Put each substance in two different cans. Tape the lids shut.

Invite the children to shake the cans and listen carefully to the sounds. Let them try to match pairs of cans according to the sounds they make. You might put some of the following in the cans:

- sand
- flour
- beans
- cotton balls
- marbles
- noodles
- paper clips
- rubber bands
- water

Remove the tape at the end of the game so that the children can check how well they matched the pairs.

Expressing Love

Purpose:

- To help children communicate love for others
- To encourage positive feelings associated with the child's giving of himself
- To help focus on how others express love to them

Materials:

- Construction paper
- Crayons or markers

Activity:

On birthdays or special occasions, make personalized cards with the children. Fold a sheet of paper in half. On the top of the outside, either you or the children may print the name of the person to be honored. Have the children draw a picture of that person under the name.

Discuss the person to be honored with the child. Elicit facts about that person or feelings the child has for him or her. Inside the card, write down what the child says. You might want to ask the child:

- "How does _____ _____ show you he loves you?"
- "How do you feel about _____?"
- "What kinds of things do you do with _____?"

Let the children illustrate the writing inside the card by drawing a scene or "describing" their feelings with their crayons. A young child's "scribbling" is packed with emotion and may express a great deal even though the picture may look like a "scramble" to the adult eye.

Many Ways To Say "I Love You"

Purpose:

● To help children understand that love is expressed in many different ways

Materials:

● None

Activity:

Discuss with the children various ways love is expressed by them or to them.

Then, invite the children to pretend they are with someone they love. Encourage them to express their feelings toward this pretend person. Some examples of how they show their love might be:
● Straightening room
● Helping wash the dishes
● Making something for them
● Giving hugs
● Telling the person, "I love you. I like being with you."
● Telling the person why they love him/her

Showing People You Love Them

Purpose:

- To help children express their positive feelings of love: verbally, physically, and by action

Materials:

- Butter
- Vanilla
- Light corn syrup
- Salt
- Powdered sugar

Activity:

Explore with the child the feelings associated with expressing love. You may indicate that there are many ways to show or tell someone how much you care for them. Ask the child for some common expressions of love. Possible suggestions are: saying I love you, hugging or kissing, or helping people with clean-up, grocery shopping, or setting the table.

It is important to show people your positive feelings. One way, for any day of the year, is by making a special treat. Here is an easy no bake candy recipe to make with the child for someone he/she loves.

No Cook Dandy Candy

Put 2 tablespoons of butter in a bowl. Add 1 tablespoon of syrup, ½ teaspoon of vanilla, 4 little pinches of salt, and stir. Then add 1 cup of powdered sugar and stir. Put the dough on a cutting board. Round it, squeeze it, and roll it. Take a small piece and roll it between your hands to make a ball as big as a walnut. Put them on a dish and enjoy!

I Trust You

Purpose:

- To help children see that working in union requires trust in one another

Materials:

- None

Activity:

Group the children in pairs. Invite them to sit on the floor, facing each other and holding hands. Play the Row Boat Game: one person pulls, while the other moves with him as they rock back and forth. Explain that in order to play this "Row Boat Game," the children must work together and trust the other person to hold hands.

Showing Mom We Love Her

Purpose:

● To help children feel the richness of creating something for a loved one

Materials:

● Waxpaper
● Flowers
● Iron

Activity:

Ask the children how they feel when they receive a gift and encourage them to give examples. Tell them they can make special gifts for their Moms that express their love.

Go outside and pick flowers, leaves, and other attractive vegetation, or bring some flowers into the class from another source, such as a home garden or store, if no flowers are accessible to the school. Press the flowers in between two pieces of waxpaper and iron them. The results are lovely mats that could be used as place mats. These gifts could be made for Mother's Day, a time set aside specially to show our love for our Moms!

It Feels Funny To Laugh

Purpose:

- To experience the joy of laughter

Materials:

- None

Activity:

Ask the children to talk about what kinds of things make them laugh and encourage them to discuss how they feel when they laugh.

Tell them they will play a Laughing Game and enjoy the feeling of laughing. The children form a human chain by lying on their backs, with each child resting his/her head on the stomach of someone else. The first child in the chain says, "ha;" the second child in the chain says, "ha,ha;" the third, "ha, ha, ha,"and so on. Before very long, hilarity occurs!

Making Noise

Purpose:

- To help children feel the power of their own bodies

Materials:

- Paper towel tubes of cardboard
- Tin pie plates
- Spoons

Activity:

Tell the children that sometimes it feels good just to make a lot of noise. Invite the children to have a Noise Party by experimenting with homemade instruments. For instance, they could bang on tin pie plates with spoons. They could also paint cardboard tubes from paper towels and blow them as horns.

Encourage the children to use these objects with abandon and joy!

It's Fun To Make A Mess

Purpose:

● To help children see that, under certain circumstances, making a mess is fine
● To encourage children to let go and feel free to explore materials in a carefully constructed environment

Materials:

● Earth
● Water
● Water or sand toys
● Water table or deep basins
● Smocks
● Old spices
● Powder

Activity:

Making a mess can be great fun for children within a carefully thought-out environment. Provide the children with earth, water and play toys in either a water table or deep basin and invite them to explore freely.

Be sure to discuss some basic rules concerning where the children may make the mess. It might be a good idea to send a note home with the children in advance alerting the parents that on that date they should dress the children for a particularly messy activity in school.

Surprise!

Purpose:

- To explore the feelings associated with being startled or surprised

Materials:

- Empty carton in which a child may crouch
- A toy jack-in-the-box

Activity:

Ask the children how they feel if someone or something jumps out at them or surprises them when they don't expect it.

Show them how the toy jack-in-the-box works and talk about the feelings of being surprised, startled, perhaps a bit scared and yet excited. Invite them to pretend to be a jack-in-the-box. One child crouches in the box and, as the group sings "Pop Goes the Weasel", he pops out at the appropriate time. Give all the children turns if they so desire.

Then encourage the group to talk about other times when they have been startled or surprised, and discuss how they felt at the time.

Hot And Cold

Purpose:

- To experience the fun of getting excited
- To explore disappointment vs. success

Materials:

- An object to hide

Activity:

Play the game "Hot and Cold." The children sit in a group. One child closes his/her eyes while another child hides an object. The first child opens his eyes and tries to find the hidden object. The group helps direct him/her by calling out "Hot" if he/she is near, and "Cold" if he/she is far from the object. The excitement mounts in the class as the searcher comes closer and closer to the goal of finding the object!

After the object is found, talk about how the children felt during the game and note how much fun it is to get excited!

Expressing Anger Constructively

Purpose:

- To help children see that we all feel angry at times
- To help children learn how to verbalize anger

Materials:

- Old mittens
- Pieces of felt or material
- Glue or needle and thread

Activity:

On one side of a pair of old mittens, glue or sew an angry face using material scraps. On the other side, attach a happy face. Ask the children to think of times they have been angry.

Invite the children to pretend that the mitten puppets are characters in one of their experiences. The children can take turns reenacting an angry scene using the puppets with the angry faces facing each other.

You might help the children express their anger verbally by saying, "Sometimes we get so angry we feel like punching. Let's use *words* to show how angry we are." OR "Are you very angry? Then, *tell* the person how angry you are."

When the conflict is resolved, turn the mittens around to allow the happy faces to achieve a warm reconciliation.

Sometimes I'm Angry And Sometimes I'm Glad

Purpose:

- To help children recognize different feelings within themselves
- To help children see that all of us feel anger and joy at various times

Materials:

- Cardboard
- Marker

Activity:

Cut two large circles out of cardboard. On one draw an angry face and on the other draw a happy face.

Have the children sit in a circle. Say, "All of us feel angry sometimes and all of us feel happy sometimes. Today, let's talk about times we've felt angry or happy."

Show the happy and angry faces. Ask the child to guess which face is happy and which face is angry. Invite the children to share with the group times they have been angry or happy. Invite them to choose the appropriate face, hold it up, and share the experience. You might also share some experiences that have made you angry or happy too.

You could end by noting again that at times we all feel angry as well as happy.

I Get So Angry When...

Purpose:

- To encourage children to get in touch with angry feelings
- To help children feel more comfortable about having angry feelings

Materials:

- Tongue depressors (or popsicle sticks)
- Crayons
- Paper plates

Activity:

Have the children look in a mirror and make an angry face. Then invite them to draw an angry face on a paper plate. Attach a tongue depressor on the back of the plate with heavy tape.

Note that sometimes we are afraid to discuss our angry feelings with people. However, there is nothing wrong with being angry and saying so.

As the children sit in a circle, encourage each one to place the angry mask in front of his/her face and complete the sentence, "I get so angry when..."

Note that anger can be expressed in constructive ways such as *telling* the person who knocked down your block building, "I am *very* angry at you." Note that in that situation words can be just as strong as punching. *And* we feel better after telling someone how angry we are.

Dealing With Anger

Purpose:

● To help children learn to express anger constructively

Materials:

● 2 big spoons flour
● 2 big spoons water
● 2 big spoons salt

Activity:

Discuss the important subject of anger with the children. You might begin by talking about things that make you angry. Ask the children to describe some of their angry moments. You might say, "How did you get your anger out?"

Discuss some of the more positive ways of expressing anger, such as talking, hitting a pillow if necessary, etc.

Sometimes it takes time for angry feelings to go away. One way of working out those remaining feelings is by making "Clobber Clay".

Clobber Clay
Mix: 2 big spoons flour
2 big spoons salt
2 big spoons water

invite the children to punch it, squeeze it, ram it on the table. This is a positive way to work out anger.

This clay may be kept in a plastic container or plastic bag and can be used over and over—especially during angry times.

I Love You Even When I'm Angry

Purpose:

- To reassure children that parents love them even when they're angry
- To allay possible fears of abandonment when parents are angry

Materials:

- Old socks
- Magic markers

Activity:

Make hand puppets by using magic markers to draw features on old socks. These socks can be used as a mitt to act out feelings.

Discuss with the children examples of times of tension and anger in their homes. Using two sock hand puppets each, the children may role-play some of the situations in which they have altercations with a parent. Talk about how the children feel when a parent is angry at them, and go into ways the conflict has been resolved. You might add that sometimes we like to be held or played with after a big argument because it makes us feel safe again. Also, you could add that anger is something we all feel sometimes. These angry feelings do *not* mean we don't love the other person—they just mean we don't feel particularly *loving* at the moment.

I'm Angry!

Purpose:

- To help children cope with their anger

Materials:

- Rags

- Old pillow case

Activity:

Stuff an old pillow case with rags and tie it closed. When children feel at loose ends with anger, invite them to wrestle with or punch this bag to release their tension. This activity should *not* be used as a substitute for conflict resolution. When children feel angry at others, they should be encouraged to verbalize this anger. Young children need to see that anger can be expressed in words rather than physical assault on another person. This bag may be used as a release when the child still feels wound up or consumed by angry energy.

Mean Words Hurt

Purpose:

- To help children understand that mean words make people feel sad
- To help children see that we all feel sad or angry when others are mean to us

Materials:

- Flannel board
- Cardboard
- Tape
- Flannel
- Flannel or felt figures

Activity:

Ask the children, "Have any of you ever been called names?" "Have other people said mean things to you?"

Encourage the children to talk about their personal experiences, noting how they felt when these incidents occured. Also, ask if the *children* have ever said mean things to others. How did they feel and how did they think the other person felt?

Invite the children to use felt figures on a flannel board to act out some of these scenes.

Feeling Disappointed

Purpose:

- To learn that sometimes disappointment is inevitable
- To see that we all experience disappointment
- To help children learn to cope with disappointment

Materials:

- Empty gift box lid

Activity:

Ask the children to mention times when they have felt disappointed, that is , when an experience did not have as happy an outcome as expected. Examples might include:

- a picnic ruined by rain
- gift clothing being too small
- a store is closed just as you get there
- a parent is detained and cannot take you out as planned
- a picture you are making turns out to be less than you expected

Then encourage the children to relate experiences which *have* had happy or satisfying outcomes.

Then tell the children you have a make-believe box filled with millions of things. Each child opens it and pretends first there is something disappointing in it and then something exciting. If a child has trouble imagining anything disappointing, you may help by saying to him/her: "Oh my, look, you have a great big onion as your present! Are you happy or disappointed?" Then say, "Let's try again." Say, "Wow, now your present is a brand new bicycle! Are you still disappointed?"

Stress that moments of disappointment are inevitable, but that so are moments of pure joy.

Learning Takes Practice

Purpose:

- To help children understand that difficult tasks seem easier with practice

Materials:

- Masking tape

Activity:

Discuss with the children tasks or activities they can perform easily. Some examples might be:

- skating
- walking
- bicycling
- balancing blocks
- reading letters
- skipping
- pouring liquids
- cutting with scissors
- whistling

These tasks at one time may have been difficult for them. Learning takes practice. Note that we all learn differently; what is easy for one person might take more practice for another.

Now place a long line of masking tape on the floor. Let the children pretend they are gymnasts or circus performers. Encourage the children first to walk across the tape, then jump, then skip or hop.

Talk about how they feel as they practice these activities on the tape. Note how much easier the task seems after they have tried it several times.

Practicing Patience: A Fishing Game

Purpose:

- To help children develop the ability to be patient
- To encourage perserverance

Materials:

- Paper clips
- Horseshoe magnet
- String
- 5 2" cardboard squares
- Basket or bag

Activity:

Attach paper clips to 5 cardboard pieces about 2" square. Draw a fish on each one.

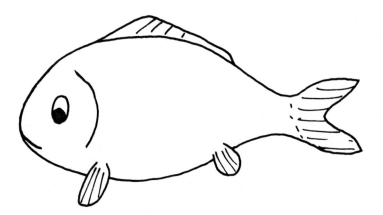

Place the cardboard fish into a basket or bag. Put in extra fish without paper clips to make the task more difficult. Tie a string to a horseshoe magnet and, one at a time, let each child try to catch a fish.

Each time a child is successful, add a blank card to the 'pool'. As the child works at the task, you might say, "Sometimes we have to wait and work a while before we get what we want. We have to be patient."

End the game after a successful catch.

82

It's Hard To Wait

Purpose:

- To help children learn that sometimes we must wait for people to pay attention to us
- To help make waiting more pleasant

Materials:

- Material
- Yarn
- Small objects described below

Activity:

Say to the children, "There are times when we must wait for someone to pay attention to us or to take our turn. Let's think of some times when we have had to wait in the classroom, at home or some place else." Some examples could be a doctor's or dentist's waiting room, grocery store, gas station, etc.

Ask the children how they feel when they must wait. Note that the waiting time seems to go faster if they are busy doing something. Tell the children they will make a special waiting bag that will have toys to be used only on special outings during which they must wait.

The waiting bag can be made by folding over a large piece of material, stitching the side and bottom and tacking on some yarn for the strap. Burlap is inexpensive, comes in wonderful colors and can be easily sewn with large needles using a basic running stitch. The children should be able to sew this material with some help from you.

Talk about what the children could keep in the bag for special waiting times. They may include crayons, paper, pipe cleaners, small story books, small cars or trucks, plastic people or animals and small blocks. As a starter you might make some play dough (1 C. flour, 1 C. water, 1 C. salt) and let each child keep some in his/her waiting bag sealed in a plastic bag.

Attach a note to the bag addressed to the parents that explains the purpose of the waiting bag. Include a list of suggestions of items or activities that would entertain the children when they are caught in a situation in which they must wait.

This is also an excellent activity to do prior to summer vacations. Children can be amused for long periods of time while traveling in cars or airplanes with their waiting bags.

I Need To Be Alone

Purpose:

• To respond to each person's need to have a private place

Materials:

• Large box or rug remnant

Activity:

A bustling class or busy home is stimulating and exciting, but there are times when each of us, including the young child, needs to retreat to a quiet, private space.

Arrange part of your room in such a way as to accommodate a small, cozy place in which a young person might find privacy. This cozy spot could be a personal cubby for each child if you have enough room. Otherwise, you might use an out-of-the-way place such as a loft or a corner. Keep books or other "quiet" materials nearby. Such a quiet spot ensures that when a child feels a need to be alone, he/she may do so and yet still feel a link with the rest of the group.

My Dream Book

Purpose:

- To help children learn that everyone dreams
- To help children see the difference between reality and fantasy with the help of a warm adult
- To lessen fears created by nightmares

Materials:

- Paper
- Crayons
- Stapler

Activity:

Discuss dreams openly with the children. Encourage them to talk about their dreams and share some of yours. Be sure not to laugh at dream-stories related by the children.

Invite the children to make a book called, "My Dream Book." Have them draw pictures that express some of their dreams. Remember, scribbling can be most expressive, even if not clear to the adult eye. Encourage the children to describe the illustrated dream and write out their description for them on the picture itself or another sheet. Staple the pages together with a title page labeled, "My Dream Book by _____"(child's name).

Fears

Young children often exhibit many fears at different stages in their development. For example, a child who might have previously enjoyed taking a bath each night may suddenly develop a fear of "falling through the drain." These fears occur because children's limited knowledge of their environment makes many events seem quite strange to them. They have difficulty anticipating the sequence of events and are often confused about cause and effect relationships.

The activities described here attempt to relieve fears by:

- Discussing these feelings in order to discover that other children experience similar concerns;
- Making the unknown familiar through experience (i.e., a visit to the doctor's office) or dramatic play (i.e., pretending to be nighttime) or explanation (i.e., understanding that while Mom sometimes has to go away, she always comes back).
- Planning a routine to be followed in the event of a troubling situation (i.e., a new baby).

Fear Of Falling Through The Drain

Purpose:

- To lessen children's fear of taking a bath by gaining a better understanding of size proportions

Materials:

- Bath toys
- Small objects from the classroom
- Collander
- Tub to catch water
- Bucket or jar of water

Activity:

Have the children examine a collander noting the small size of the holes. Let the children experiment pouring water through a collander. Place some objects from the classroom in the collander and ask the children what they think will happen to the items when water is poured over them. Encourage them to experiment with various objects and water. You might ask, "Why didn't the object fall through the holes?"

Note that the holes in the collander are like the bathtub drain: water can flow through, but objects and people cannot.

If there is access to a drain (outside, or in a sink or tub) repeat this game using water, the objects and the collander.

Sounds Of The Night

Purpose:

- To lessen childrens' fear of the dark at nighttime

Materials:

- Tape recorder
- Tape with night sounds

Activity:

Discuss with the children the various everyday sounds you hear. They may include:

- traffic sounds outside
- creaking floors
- noisy neighbors
- toilet flushing
- telephone ringing
- window rattling
- dog barking
- cat screeching
- furnace or refrigerator buzzing
- snow falling
- wind blowing
- bed creaking

Tape record these sounds and in the light of day listen to them. Let the children guess what sounds they are hearing.

Darken the room and play the tape again while the children pretend to go to sleep. Note that the same sounds occur in the night as well as the day. These sounds are natural and will be less frightening to the children when they become more familiar with them.

Lighting Up The Dark

Purpose:

- To help children feel more comfortable in the dark

Material:

- Flashlight

Activity:

Sit with the children in the classroom and look around and note where various objects are. Turn off the lights (but don't make the room pitch black) and see if the children can remember where the objects are. Have them use a flashlight to point to a spot. Point out to the group that things you see in the light are still there, even though it may be dark and we cannot see them too clearly.

In the home, parents can play this game with children as they lie in bed at night. The fearful child might feel comfortable keeping the flashlight available during the night as a reassurance that things don't disappear in the dark and they themselves can control the darkness.

Fear Of The Dark

Purpose:

● To help children deal with anxiety about the dark and going to sleep at night

Materials:

● 1 sheet each of white and black crepe paper
● 3 chairs
● Tape

Activity:

Tape the crepe paper sheets between the chairs to form a double curtain:

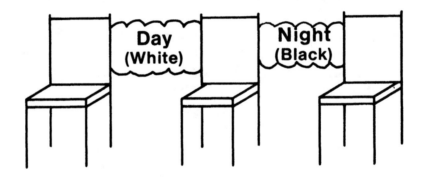

Explain to the children the "Day and Night" game. The area of the white paper is day and the area of the black paper is night.

Let the children sit in the "day" area, and pretend to go through various daytime experiences, such as eating, shopping, watching T.V., playing outside.

Then indicate that it is getting dark and encourage them to move to the area of the black paper. Pretend to go through experiences associated with nighttime and bed time, e.g., brushing teeth, reading a story, getting a favorite toy or a glass of water. Discuss how the nighttime is different. Feel free to step back as the children become involved in the creative play.

Then note that even though it gets dark and things seem different, everything really stays the same. The room is the same, the toys are the same, and most important, Mom and/or Dad are the same, and will be there to love and take care of their children.

92

Fears At Nighttime

Purpose:

- To help children deal with fears associated with the nighttime

Materials:

- White chalk
- Black construction paper

Activity:

Encourage the children to discuss any fears they might have during the nighttime. Explain that in the dark, fears sometimes feel scarier, but Mom and/or Dad are there to love and care for their children.

Invite the children to use the white chalk on the black construction paper to express some of their nighttime fears.

I Can't See You But I Know You're There

Purpose:

- To reassure young children of a parent's reappearance
- To show that separations are part of everyday life

Materials:

- A scarf or piece of material large enough to cover one's head

Activity:

Play a simple peek-a-boo game with the children by placing a scarf over your face, saying: "Where am I?" Then whisk it off jokingly and cry: "Peek-a-boo, here I am!"

Then encourage the children to talk about times a parent leaves and then later returns. Instances could include parents' leaving for work, sporting events, meetings, trips or shopping. Note that even though it sometimes makes you sad to let go when your parent has to leave you, each time he/she *does* come home.

Invite the children to role-play some of the examples they have experienced firsthand.

Sometimes I Feel Scared

Purpose:

- To help children see that everyone feels scared sometimes
- To help children deal with some of their fears

Materials:

- Large paper or catalog

Activity:

Talk about how we all feel scared sometimes and offer several examples, such as:

- being in a new place
- nighttime
- nightmares
- meeting new people
- being alone

Note that when we talk about what we fear, we don't feel alone anymore.

Discuss ways we might resolve and ease some of these fears and act them out. Examples might include:

- A night light makes the dark a bit lighter and less inky.
- Holding a friend's hand makes you feel safe when you meet someone new.
- Taking a precious doll or stuffed friend when you sleep away from home makes the new bed feel not so new.

Then you might wish to make an experience chart illustrating some ways we ease our fears.

I'm Lost!

Purpose:

- To explore feelings associated with being lost
- To help children learn how to deal with being lost

Materials:

- None

Activity:

Ask the children if they have ever been lost. Encourage them to share how they felt. What did they do? Ask the children who might help them find their way home or locate a parent in a crowd. Would a police officer help? What would you say to the officer?

Role-play some situations that the children have experienced or imagined. One child would be a police officer and wear a hat and badge, and another child would be the lost person. You could further discuss the importance of knowing one's telephone number and address when one is lost. To add a note of reassurance, tell the children that there *are* people in our neighborhood who can help us when we are lost or have some questions, and that we are not really alone.

Feeling Sick

Purpose:

- To deal with the anxiety and discomfort of feeling sick

Materials:

- Doll

Activity:

Talk with the child about how unhappy we all feel sometimes when we're sick. Then, discuss with the child some ways to feel a little better and more comfortable when ill. Some examples might be an alcohol rub, medicine, jello or soup, newly made playdough, books, a radio in the room, or quiet singing by Mom or Dad. Pretend a doll is sick and encourage the child to care for the doll by doing some of the special things you might do to ease the discomfort and unhappy feelings.

When going to the doctor, let the child take the special doll and invite the doctor to treat it also.

Sometimes Parents Have to Say Goodbye

Purpose:

- To help children accept the fact that parents leave and then return

Materials:

- None

Activity:

Ask the children to talk about times their parents have left them for a while. Ask, "How do you feel when they leave? Do you sometimes feel angry? Do you sometimes try to make them stay?"

Then ask, "How do you feel when they return?"

Explain that all grown-ups need to do grown-up things by themselves. But even so, they still love their children and always return.

Encourage the children to role-play situations when their parents leave them for a while. Some examples might be:

- parents go to work
- parents go shopping
- parents go out in the evening
- parents go on vacation

Baby Pictures

Purpose:

- To help children understand that we were all babies at one time

Materials:

- Photograph pictures from home

Activity:

Send a note home to parents asking for two pictures: one a recent photograph of the child, and the other a baby picture.

Have the children show and share their pictures. It would be fun for teachers to also share baby pictures of themselves.

Note that we were all babies at one time and point out the amazing changes that have occurred since then. Mix up the pictures and have the children pair up the baby pictures with the recent pictures. Have the children discuss similarities and differences between the two.

A New Baby In The House

Purpose:

- To help develop a nurturing feeling for a new baby

Materials:

- Basins
- Washable dolls
- Baby bottles
- Cloths for washing and drying

Activity:

Invite to the classroom a mother and father with their young baby. Have the children watch as they feed, bathe and dress and generally take care for the baby. Point out to the children that by taking care of the baby in these ways, we show the baby how much we love and care for him.

Then invite the children to care for the "babies" or dolls in the class. Have available basins, cloths, little blankets, bottles, etc.

Preschool children often experience a new birth in their immediate families. Having this type of imaginative play available to the young children at these times can be most satisfying for them.

Sibling Rivalry

Purpose:

- To ease young children's resentment about a baby in the family by encouraging their identification with a nurturing adult

Materials:

- Bag or sack (an old pillowcase, purse, shopping bag, canvas bag)
- "Baby equipment" used by Mom/Dad; e.g., Pampers/diapers, cotton balls, powder, bottle, receiving blanket, etc.
- Old baby clothes
- A doll or stuffed animal

Activity:

Gather equipment for children to use to "pretend" to care for a baby. Keep these materials together in an easily accessible place such as in a bag. Boys as well as girls find satisfaction in being nurturant and loving; they feel, in turn, loved and cared for.

Encourage the children to draw pictures of someone they love. Let them relate a story about this person while you write down the words under the pictures.

Coping with Divorce I:
Expressing Feelings

Purpose:

● To help children cope with feelings associated with a divorce

Materials:

● Clay

Activity:

Sometimes when a child in the group is involved in a divorce process at home, he/she experiences difficulty in the school setting.

We might see physical clues such as aggression or withdrawal, or we might hear the child verbally articulate anger, sadness, fear of abandonment, self-blame, or other feelings. At this time, a sympathetic and trusted adult may want to encourage the child to talk about his/her feelings and to use clay to express these emotions. The child might feel comfortable being able to express his/her rage and fear in a controlled setting using this mound of clay that is malleable and yet resistant.

Coping With Divorce II: Feeling Love And Reassurance

Purpose:

- To help children feel reassured that parents continue to love them after a divorce
- To help children understand that they are not to blame for the breakup of their parents' marriage

Materials:

- Construction Paper
- Staples
- Crayons

Activity:

When parents go through a divorce, children may feel, among other things, that they will not be loved as they were before the divorce. Further, sometimes they feel that they caused the breakup. These young children need to be reassured that:

- their parents will continue to love them, and
- the breakup was not due to the children's behavior, but rather to issues existing wholly between the parents.

You may help a particular child in these circumstances by inviting him/her to think of "ways my Mom and Dad love me." Encourage the child to talk about fun and sharing times he/she has with either parent. Write down what the child says and let him/her illustrate the pages as you read them back to him/her. Staple them together into a special scrapbook.

Emphasize to the child that the loving, closeness, fun and sharing he/she enjoys with both parents will continue even after the divorce, and the loving feelings his/her parents have for him/her will not disappear but will *still* be there.

NOTE: This activity would best be done *on an individual* basis, rather than as a group project, to protect other children from undue fantasizing and worrying about the solidity of their own parents' marriages.

My Mom's In The Hospital

Purpose:

- To ease the loneliness and void felt when a child is separated from a parent due to hospitalization
- To reassure the young child that the parent really still exists even though the two are separated

Materials:

- Thin notebook
- Crayons

Activity:

Develop an ongoing story between the hospitalized parent and child who remains at home. The parent begins a story, writes it in a notebook, and gives it to a visitor to return it home. The child reads (or is read) the story written and then adds more. The child might then illustrate the story. Return the notebook back to the hospitalized parent, who adds to the story, and then sends it back to the child. The adult or older sibling helping the young child might need to ask questions to aid the child in continuing the story. When recording the child's contribution to the story, write down the child's own words. Continue this procedure until the story is finished. If desired, the parent and child may start a new story.

Dealing With A Long-Term Separation

Purpose:

- To help young children cope with a long-term separation of a parent due to illness, hospitalization, imprisonment or any similar experience

Materials:

- Paper
- Crayons

Activity:

On an individual basis, a trusted adult (parent, guardian, teacher, etc.) should encourage the child to open up and describe the anger, fear, loneliness and other feelings associated with a long-term separation. Sometimes children feel less alone with their scary, angry feelings when an adult shares the feelings with them.

Then give the child some crayons and paper and say, "Use the crayons to show these feelings."

Discuss with the child the colors, objects, or design of the picture and how it feels to color out these feelings.

I Have To Have An Operation

Purpose:

● To help children deal with an operation

Materials:

● None

Activity:

With the children, look through a picture book that deals with hospitalization and talk about:

● aspects of the experience and how the story characters might be feeling as they move through the experience
● feelings experienced by the children themselves

Then, encourage the children to act out various aspects of the hospital experience. You might include:
● checking in (discuss what the children might need to bring)
● taking medicine to help them sleep
● gentle waking up
● bandaging
● getting dressed and going home

I Hurt My Leg

Purpose:

- To experience how one feels and copes with a leg injury
- To develop empathy for those who must cope with limited leg movement

Materials:

- Gauze
- Rod, stick, dowel or ruler

Activity:

Ask the children if any of them has ever hurt or broken his/her leg or knows of anyone else who has. Encourage them to share what the experience was like.

Tell the children they are going to pretend they broke their leg and must wear a cast to keep it from moving while it heals. Place a rigid rod, such as a ruler or dowel, next to the child's leg and keep it in place by wrapping gauze around it.

Invite the children to move about and play with their "casts" on. Encourage the children to talk about the difficulty they encounter, the solutions they think of and the feelings they experience. Encourage the children to help each other as they see each other in need.

I Hurt My Arm

Purpose:

- To experience how one feels and copes with an arm injury
- To develop empathy for those who function with limited arm movement

Materials:

- Scarves

Activity:

Ask the group if anyone has hurt or broken his/her arm, or if any of them knows of anyone who has suffered in this way. Ask these children to share what the experience was like.

Tell the children they are going to pretend they hurt their arms. To protect the hurt arm, they must keep it in a sling. Tie a scarf over each child's shoulder and slip an arm into this "sling."

Invite the children to try various tasks with their arms immobilized. You might try:

- tying shoes
- buttoning coat
- pouring juice
- crayoning
- reading a book
- building with blocks
- taking a puzzle apart

Discuss the difficulties they encounter, the feelings they experience, such as frustration and impatience, and the solutions they come up with to successfully carry out these activities. To heighten the children's sensitivities, encourage them to help each other.

My World Around Me

Children's first experiences occur in the home and it is here that they begin to acquire a positive self-image. As they become more aware of themselves as individuals, they begin to turn their interests outward and, through personal involvement, to develop a growing sense of their environment and social responsibility. When children venture into the community, they come into contact with many adults of different occupations. By helping them develop an understanding of the services these people provide, parents and teachers help the children become more knowledgeable about and comfortable with their environment. In addition, the knowledge that there are other trusted adults in their community, such as firefighters and police officers, who are ready to help them if necessary, fosters in children a sense of security with others outside of their immediate home.

The activities described in this section build on the child's growing sense of self in an ever-enlarging environment. Activities which allow the children to explore the home, the community and the natural environment encourage children to clarify their world and integrate it into their own understanding.

My Room

Purpose:

- To encourage children to view their "ordinary" world as rich in texture and excitement
- To develop children's curiosity in the world around them and to give them confidence in exploring their world

Materials:

- Paper
- Crayons
- Cardboard
- Glue

Activity:

Take rubbings of objects throughout the classroom or bedroom by placing a piece of paper over an object and rubbing the paper with a crayon. Ordinary objects become exciting as the children explore their varying textures and appearances by viewing them in this unusual manner.

Once the children become comfortable with the method, they can explore the textures of many objects in the room. Then each child can make a collage of these rubbings by gluing them onto cardboard however they please.

Building My Family

Purpose:

● To help children understand their relationship with other family members

Materials:

● Small boxes, such as small cereal boxes
● Construction paper
● Crayons or markers

Activity:

Talk with the children about how a family grows, from grandparents to parents and then to you, the children. Ask each child to name his/her grandparents, parents and siblings. Tell the children they are going to make family blocks. Wrap construction paper around small boxes. Tape or glue the boxes shut. Have the children draw one family member on each covered box. Help them build their family pyramid by using the grandparent figures as a base, balancing the parent figures on top of them, and then placing the children's and their siblings' figures on top of the parents.

Family Houses

Purpose:

- To help children realize that people live in many different kinds of homes
- To help children see that homes fulfill certain needs of living

Materials:

- Flannel
- Cardboard
- Tape
- Scraps of felt

Activity:

Show pictures of different types of homes: apartment houses, single family units, huts, igloos, trailers, houseboats, and tents. Discuss why people live in these types of houses. What needs do they have?

Have the children describe their own homes. Talk about how their homes fulfill certain needs, such as keeping the wind and rain out, keeping the family warm in winter, etc.

Make flannel boards by covering heavy cardboard with a piece of flannel and taping it to the back.

Encourage the children to depict their homes on the flannel board using scraps of felt material of varied shapes and sizes.

Who Lives In Your Home?

Purpose:

- To help children become more aware of their own families as well as the families of their peers
- To help children see how family members help each other, live with each other, and are related to each other
- To help children understand that sometimes nonrelatives share a home, too

Materials:

- Construction paper
- Crayons
- Stapler

Activity:

Have each child bring to class a photograph of all the people who live in the child's home. Encourage each child to name all the people and tell how they are related.

Have each child make a scrapbook entitled, "The People In My Home." Staple construction paper together. Print the title on the front page and have the child glue the photograph on. Label the following pages:

- "We Have Fun At Home."
- "We Work Together."
- "We Have Fun On Trips."
- "We Help Each Other."
- "We Sometimes Argue."

Encourage the children to think of how these aspects of living apply to their life at home. Write down what the children say, and have them illustrate each page with drawings.

Show and Share: Learning About Family Members

Purpose:

- To encourage children to think about the members of their family

Materials:

- None

Activity:

Have the children bring to school objects that make them think about each member of their families. Have them show these objects to the rest of the group. Encourage the children to explain how the family member uses the object, or why the object reminds them of that person. Also, encourage the children to express how that object makes them feel about the relative. As an example, a baby sister's bottle might remind a child that sometimes the child wishes he/she were still a baby too.

My Family Helps Each Other

Purpose:

- To help children realize and verbalize how family members help each other
- To help children gain a sense of the needs of others in the family

Materials:

- None

Activity:

Discuss with the children different ways family members help each other. Invite the children to pretend they are various members of their family and role-play some of these situations. You might include experiences such as:

- cleaning house
- caring for an ill person
- caring for an infant
- caring for an elderly person
- preparing food
- getting and giving a haircut
- helping an injured family member
- learning to ride a bike
- helping with homework

Point out to the children that we all need help sometimes—even adults—and the people in our family care about each other and want to give each other the help we sometimes need.

Family Time Is Sharing Time

Purpose:

- To help children feel secure in belonging to a group of people, the family, that shares warm times together

Materials:

- Heavy paper
- Crayons
- Glue
- Scissors

Activity:

Ask the children how their family spends time together in shared activities. Encourage them to discuss what they enjoy doing with their families. Ideas could include eating meals together, cooking together, doing yard work or housecleaning, engaging in hobbies, taking walks, reading, playing games, going to church or synagogue.

Invite the children to make finger puppets of family members by cutting little figures out of heavy paper and decorating them with crayons or glued pieces of paper. Make 2 parallel, horizontal slits in the puppet's body to fit the fingers through as shown below:

Encourage the children to use these family puppets on long trips when they share experiences with their family.

Encourage the children to verbalize how they feel when their families share activities.

My Home: Block Play

Purpose:

● To give children an opportunity to explore concretely the dimensions of their home-life experience

Materials:

● Blocks and associated materials that enhance dramatic play

Activity:

Encourage the children to talk about their home environment. You might help spark the discussion by posing some of the following questions:

● "What are some of the different rooms in your home?"
● "What do people do in the different rooms?"
● "What parts of your home do you like best?"
● "Where are quiet places? Where are noisy places?"

Invite the children to use blocks to construct their homes. Offer an assortment of materials to the children and encourage them to use imaginative play as they pretend the block constructions are their homes.

Adjunct material could include:
● wood, rubber, or paper doll figures
● vehicles
● wood or rubber animals
● traffic signs
● doll furniture
● small pieces of oddly-shaped wood
● material scraps, including small rug pieces
● beads

My Cookie Family

Purpose:

- To help children view themselves as part of a larger unit
- To help children see, focus on, and articulate the specialness of their family members

Materials:

- Refrigerator cookie dough
- Cookie cutters
- Cake-decorating tidbits
- Rolling pin

Activities:

Soften refrigerator cookie dough. Slice some off and roll it out. Cut out figures representing the child's family members using gingerbread man cookie cutters or cardboard human figures. Discuss with the children specific features representative of the various family members and decorate the cookies accordingly. For instance, the children might "individualize" the cookies by decorating them with a particular eye color, curly hair, mustache, glasses, favorite sweater, nail polish, etc.

Use sprinkles, raisins, nuts, colored icing drawn with tooth picks or spread with hands or tongue depressors, chocolate bits, or fork/knife indentations for decorating the cookies. Painting with food coloring is also fun.

Away From Home

Purpose:

- To help prepare children for an overnight visit away from home, and to ease some of the apprehension of separation

Materials:

- Small suitcase or shopping bag
- Appropriate nighttime gear; e.g., pajamas, slippers, toothbrush, special teddy, etc.
- Card table or 4 chairs
- Sheet

Activity:

Discuss with the child what is needed for an overnight visit. Help pack these few things in a small suitcase or bag.

Place a sheet over a card table or 4 chairs, forming a square. Pretend the interior space is the place to be visited. You may pretend to bring the child to the new place, stay and play awhile, then kiss goodbye. Reassure the child that you will return. Then, after your child spends some time "visiting", return to pick him/her up and go home together.

Family Portrait

Purpose:

- To help children see that they are part of a family group

Materials:

- Crayons
- Paper
- Cardboard
- Plastic wrap

Activity:

Have the children draw a picture of their family. Ask each child to name the people pictured and label them (with your help, if necessary). Scribbles and mis-proportioned people are all part of the young child's perception. Pets may be included in the children's view of their family group. Sometimes a sibling is "forgotten"—perhaps due to some wishful thinking?

To make the picture more permanent, mount it within a cardboard frame and cover it with plastic wrap, taped in place on the back.

Inside My Home

Purpose:

- To help children feel secure that their homes fulfill their needs of daily living

Materials:

- Large construction paper
- Magazines
- Crayons
- Glue

Activity:

Ask the children to draw a large picture of their home. Invite them to cut out magazine pictures of objects they use in their home and glue them onto the house they've drawn. They could also draw in any other objects that come to mind. Talk about how our homes are places where our parents take care of us. In our homes, we have many things that help us be happy, healthy, and comfortable.

Starting School

Purpose:

- To make the child feel more comfortable about beginning school
- To help ease separation anxiety that may be felt even though school is not an entirely new experience

Materials:

- Photograph of family

Activity:

There are several activities that can ease the separation anxiety associated with a new school experience.

- Tape a photograph of the child's family to the inside lid of his/her lunch box.
- Walk or ride to the child's new school before school begins so it is not an unfamiliar experience.
- Visit the school and the teacher if possible.
- Take a ride on the school bus with the child.
- See if the school is open to home visits by the teacher.
- Place little notes in the child's lunchbox—a comforting surprise at midday.
- Make preparing lunch and packing the lunchbox a time of shared activity with the child.

Our School Family

Purpose:

- To help children view their class as a familial group

Material:

- Photographs of the children
- Butcher paper
- Paint

Activity:

Have the children bring a photograph of themselves to school. Discuss how the class is like a family or group. Some possible ways to develop the concept are as follows:

- The teachers care for the children as parents do
- The teacher and the children play together
- They work together
- They eat and rest together
- They sometimes argue
- They take trips together

Tell the children they will make a big picture of their school family.

Draw the outline of a large house on butcher paper. Have the children paint it together. Then invite them to glue their photographs on.

The Community

We All Need Help Sometimes

Purpose:

- To encourage children to cooperate with each other

Materials:

- None

Activity:

Ask the children to talk about activities that require cooperative action. Some possible examples are:

- riding a seesaw
- being pushed on a swing
- putting on a coat
- tying shoe laces
- holding a cup to be poured into
- carrying large blocks
- holding water fountain while another drinks

Place the children in pairs and have them try some of these cooperative activities and tasks. Encourage them to verbalize their feelings as they work together, and comment encouragingly when the pairs show cooperative actions. You might say, for instance, "You two move so beautifully together to make the seesaw work!" Or "How does it feel to have John hold the water fountain for you? Is it just as easy to drink and hold it for yourself?"

The People Who Help Me

Purpose:

- To encourage children to feel comfortable with other adults

Materials:

- Large sheets of paper
- Paint

Activity:

Encourage the children to talk about people in their lives in whom they place trust and on whom they can rely. You might help by asking:

- "Who in your home, school or elsewhere helps you?"
- "How do they help you?"
- "When you are sick, who takes care of you?"
- "When you need to cross a busy street, who helps you?"
- "When your parents go out, who takes good care of you?"
- "What do you do with your baby sitter?"

Some examples of such people are, of course, parents, siblings, other relatives, baby sitters, police officers, teachers and clergy.

Invite the children to use paint and paper to depict some of these adult friends. Then label them on the paper for the children so they have pictorial representations of trusting and trustworthy adults in their lives.

Community Helpers

Purpose:

- To offer children opportunities to broaden their understanding of the roles played by workers in their neighborhood
- To enrich their dramatic play

Activity:

Most children are curious about the people who work in the neighborhood. Community workers, such as firefighters, carpenters, etc., are people that young children regard with special affection and respect. Encourage the children to discuss a community worker's role.

Collect materials in a shoebox that children can use as props when pretending to be community helpers. Cut and paste a picture of the community helper on top of the shoebox. The children will have all they need for future creative play. Some suggestions are:

- **Mail Deliverers**
  envelopes with cancelled stamps
  old magazines
  "packages"
  change purse to collect "C.O.D.'s"
  sack for letters

- **Firefighters**
  old raincoats
  caps
  old rubber boots
  flashlight
  pretend ladder

- **Emergency Medic**
  band aids
  cloth
  small blanket
  "sick" dolls or stuffed animals
  wash cloth
  thermometer cut from cardboard
  small car (as an ambulance)

The Police Officer Helps Me

Purpose:

- To help children feel comfortable and secure with police officers

Materials:

- A real police officer
- Boxes
- String
- Safety pins
- Cardboard
- Aluminum foil

Activity:

Ask the children if they know a police officer. Ask them, "What does the officer do? What does the officer wear? How does the officer help us?"

Invite a police officer to visit the class. (It is a good idea to discuss with the officer *before* his/her visit how to talk to very young children.) Encourage the officer to explain his/her uniform, badge, walkie-talkie, horse, motorcycle, car, etc. Have the officer demonstrate the badge, handcuffs, radio, gun safety, and car siren, if possible.

Provide props pertaining to the responsibilities of the police officer and encourage the children to engage in dramatic play. Some examples of homemade props are:

- badge: cover cardboard stars with aluminum foil and attach a safety pin to the back.
- walkie-talkie: paint long boxes to use as walkie-talkies or tie string between two paper cups.
- police car: arrange chairs 2 by 2 and paint a steering wheel on a paper plate.

Other props could include a flashlight, toy siren, old men's jackets or vests and caps with badges pinned on. To down play the role of guns, have the children use fingers as pretend guns rather than realistic toy guns.

Traffic Lights Help Us Be Safe

Purpose:

- To help children learn how to "read" traffic lights
- To help children understand the importance of traffic lights

Materials:

- Red and green construction paper
- Music

Activity:

Cut out large circles of red and green construction paper. Tell the children to pretend that you are a traffic light. Hold up the red circle and ask, "What does this mean?"

Hold up the green dot and ask the same question.

Then ask the children, "Why do we need traffic lights? Suppose you wanted to cross the street and there were no traffic lights. What would happen?"

Invite several children to stand at various places in the room and pretend to be traffic lights. Invite the other children to pretend to be cars and trucks; have them describe the type of vehicle they would like to be. Play some music and encourage the "traffic lights" to flash the red and green circles. Tell the "vehicles" to be very careful and obey the "traffic lights."

Handling A Fire Emergency I: A Fire Drill

Purpose:

● To teach children procedures to follow in a fire drill

Materials:

● None

Activity:

Discuss the need for a fire drill. It is important to practice how to act if we really do need to leave the building quickly.

If you have a public address system, alert the children to its loud sound and play it several times so they are not unduly startled when they hear it. If you do not have a public address system, ring a loud bell.

Talk about the procedures you expect the children to follow. They should include:

● Stop at once
● Listen to the adults and do what they say
● NO TALKING
● Come when called

Before the first drill be sure you have worked out the best escape route. Then when you hold a drill, lead the children calmly and quickly to the appropriate exit. Your first drills should be when the children expect them, but after the procedures become more familiar, have the drills at unexpected times.

You can make these drills seem important without creating worry or anxiety by down playing the possibility of fire. Stress that the drill is to practice leaving the building quickly rather than emphasizing the need to escape from a fire emergency.

Handling A Fire Emergency II: Visiting A Fire Station

Purpose:

● To acquaint children with firemen

Materials:

● Poster board
● Props for firefighter play

Activity:

Discuss with the children how the fireman helps us. Talk about the equipment and clothes firefighters use. Plan to visit a fire station. As with any trip, visit it alone beforehand and set up an appointment with the station.

When the children visit the station, explore the surroundings, equipment, tools and uniforms. When you return to class, encourage the children to discuss what they saw, felt and learned at their visit. Write the children's comments on a large sheet of poster board and read it back.

As a follow-up, have firefighter props readily available for dramatic play. You could include:

● pieces of hose
● toy hats
● old boots

You could also set up chairs and put tape on the floor to simulate a fire engine. In addition, section off an area to be a place for the firemen to rest.

Learning My Address

Purpose:

- To help children learn their addresses
- To help children feel self-reliant

Materials:

- 5" x 7" index cards
- Crayons

Activity:

On separate 5" x 7" index cards, write each child's address. Call them out individually and ask the children to tell you when they recognize their own addresses. Ask the child to repeat his/her address to you. If a child does not recognize the address, offer a hint, such as, "The person who lives here is wearing a red and yellow dress today." Continue the game until all the children can recognize their addresses.

Have them decorate their address cards. Mix them up and invite the children to pick out their own address cards. Then tape each child's card to the inside of his/her cubby.

Learning My Telephone Number

Purpose:

- To help children learn and understand the importance of their telephone numbers

Materials:

- 5" x 7" index cards
- Crayons

Activity:

Repeat the lesson for "Learning My Address," but this time use the telephone numbers of the children in class.

To further help the children learn their telephone numbers clap hands and chant rhythmically each child's telephone number. The children will enjoy learning the numbers much as they would enjoy learning a new rhythmic song.

Telephone Talk

Purpose:

- To help children learn how to use the telephone to call for help in an emergency
- To help children feel confident in handling an emergency if they have to do so

Materials:

- Piece of cardboard for each child
- String
- 2 orange juice cans

Activity:

Tell the children they are going to make toy telephones and pretend to call the police or fire department. The telephones are made by connecting two clean, empty juice cans with a long piece of string. Each child then draws a circle on a piece of cardboard and fills in the appropriate numbers:

On each child's "dial," write the number of his home, the police and the fire department. The child draws a picture of his home, a police car and a fire truck beside the appropriate number.

As a demonstration, role-play emergency situations with several children and pretend to call the appropriate number. Then invite the children to role-play together. (Step in to augment the play when necessary).

NOTE: With very young children, teach them to use "O" to dial the Operator for help rather than the appropriate telephone numbers of the fire or police department.

Mailing A Letter

Purpose:

- To help children understand the process of mailing a letter and the function of the post office as a vital aspect of their community

Materials:

- Paper
- Crayons
- Envelope

Activity:

Ask the children if they have ever received any mail. Discuss the following questions:

- "What is on the envelope?"
- "Who brings the mail?"
- "How does the mail get to you?"
- "What happens when you want to send a letter?"

Discuss the role of the post office, including stamp purchasing, sorting, and delivering. Tell the children that they are going to write a letter to their own homes. Then, as a group, they are going to take the letters to the post office to buy stamps and mail them. Invite the children to draw pictures and/or dictate a letter to someone in their home. Show the children how you write their home addresses on the envelope. Then seal each child's letter after he/she licks the envelope. When you take the trip to the post office, have each child purchase his/her stamp, paste it on his/her letter, and drop the letter in the chute. As you walk around, discuss the various aspects of the post office, taking particular note of the jobs of various workers. Don't forget to look for the trucks outside.

In a day or so, ask the children if they have received their letters.

You might have available some equipment that could stimulate post office imaginative play as a follow-up to the letter-writing experience. You might include paper, envelopes, cancelled stamps (or the children could make their own), play money, toy trucks, bags for delivery, and rubber stampers.

Getting A Haircut

Purpose:

● To help children view getting a haircut as a fun experience

Materials:

● Paper towel rolls
● Combs
● Hair brushes
● Plastic bottles
● Curlers
● Mirrors
● Net
● Sheeting
● Old hair blower
● Magazines
● Cash register

Activity:

Discuss with the children what it is like to get a haircut. Set up a pretend Barber Shop/Beauty Parlor and encourage the children to use creative play to explore this experience. Set up chairs, and put out magazines for the people to look through as they wait their turns. Use a toy cash register for "payout." Paint a cardboard paper towel tube red and white for a barber shop pole. Arrange combs, brushes, plastic bottles, curlers, mirrors, nets, clips on a tray; use sheeting for robes; use two fingers as scissors.

NOTE: Emphasize with the children that this activity involves *imaginative* play only. Real scissors should *never* be used.

BOOK: *Mop Top* by D. Freeman is an excellent resource for this activity.

The Dental Visit

Purpose:

- To familiarize children with the experience of going to the dentist

Materials:

- Dolls
- Play dough
- Popsicle sticks or tooth picks
- Small mirrors

Activity:

The following are several activities or games designed to familiarize children with the dental visit and ease some anxiety associated with the experience:

- Take the children on a trip to a dentist or if you are a parent, invite your children to come and watch you during your check-up. Be matter-of-fact and avoid emphasizing the idea that "It won't hurt at all," or "It will hurt for just a minute." These statements might elicit anxiety when there was none to begin with!
- Invite the children to play dentist using play dough. They can pretend to explore "teeth" using wooden tongue depressors, popsicle sticks or tooth picks and mirrors. The children can also use dolls as patients when playing with these dental "instruments."

Doctor's Visit

Purpose:

- To familiarize children with what a doctor does, and to acquaint them with the names and nature of commonly used medicines and instruments
- To develop understanding about injections and lessen children's fears about visiting a doctor's office
- To develop ability to play imaginatively "make-believe doctor"

Materials:

- Toy doctor's bag
- Toys such as stuffed bears, animals or dolls

Activity:

Show children the doctor's bag and ask them what it is, who uses it and what we might find inside.

Ask the children if any of them have been to the *doctor* and had an injection, and encourage them to discuss their experiences.

Show the children the doctor's bag and the dolls and stuffed animals. Tell the children these dolls/animals are "sick." Ask the children,

- "How do you feel when you are sick?"
- "How do you feel when you need an injection?"
- "Do you feel sad or angry?"
- "Does it hurt?"

Invite them to reach into the bag and take out instruments and examine the "patients." Offer suggestions such as, "This patient feels better, but let's take his temperature to make sure."

Step back once dramatic play progresses.

Keeping My Community Clean

Purpose:

- To encourage a feeling of responsibility toward and pride in one's community
- To develop a positive attitude about keeping one's neighborhood clean and beautiful

Materials:

- None

Activity:

Ask the children,

- "How does it feel when you walk through the neighborhood and see garbage thrown around?"
- "Does a messy neighborhood make you feel happy or sad? Angry? What happens when you play ball, ride a bike and there are bottles lying around?"
- "What could we do to make our neighborhood a cleaner, prettier, happier place?"

Invite the children to go on a "Litter Walk." Bring a garbage bag, walk through the neighborhood and collect refuse or neaten the area.

When you return, talk about how you all felt about making the community a better place to live and play.

Big Truck/Little Car

Purpose:

●   To encourage children to become more aware of transportation in their neighborhood

Materials:

●   Music

Activity:

Take a walk in the neighborhood and talk about vehicles that pass by. Note small and large trucks and their functions; buses; cars; and two-wheeled vehicles. Return to the classroom and discuss with the children what they have seen. Put on some music and invite them to pretend to be some of the vehicles they have seen on their neighborhood walk.

Recognizing Danger

Purpose:

- To help children learn how to recognize and deal with potentially dangerous situations in their environment
- To foster a sense of self-reliance in young children as they learn ways to recognize and handle danger signs

Materials:

- Objects or pictures of danger signals

Activity:

Collect several objects which are potentially dangerous and/or pictures of potentially dangerous situations or conditions. The pictures may be simply drawn, photographed, or clipped from newspapers or magazines. Some examples might be:

- a book of matches
- knife
- scissors
- icy street
- open window
- hot stove
- railroad tracks
- unfamiliar dog
- medicine bottle
- busy street

Show the objects and pictures you have collected to the children. Discuss how to deal with these potentially dangerous situations. Stress that the situations themselves need not be dangerous so long as we:

- know what they are,
- know what they mean, and
- know how to handle them.

Children may enjoy acting out how to proceed when encountering these dangerous situations.

Poison!

Purpose:

- To help children learn to recognize and avoid common poisons

Materials:

- Paper
- Crayons

Activity:

Talk with the children about the dangers of tasting certain things that could make us really sick. Explain that these things are called "poisons". Ask the children to name some poisons. Some common examples are:

- medicines
- moth balls
- berry bushes
- cleaning fluid
- house plants

Write down for each child on pieces of paper the poisons named in class. Invite the children to illustrate their Poisons Sheet and encourage them to take them home and talk to their parents about them.

Smells Are Clues

Purpose:

- To encourage children to be alert to smells in their own neighborhood

Materials:

- None

Activity:

While walking outside throughout the neighborhood, note the myriad of smells you encounter. Be detectives and search out the origins of the smells.

Some examples might be:

- cut grass
- gas emission for cars
- flowers
- hot, melting tar
- pine trees
- garbage
- burning leaves

Neighborhood Smells

Purpose:

- To encourage children to learn more about their community by using their senses of smell

Materials:

- None

Activity:

Visit different stores in the neighborhood. Sniff for different smells and try to locate their sources. You might try a grocery store, florist, bakery, candy store, or even a hardware store.

Neighborhood Potpourri

Purpose:

- To encourage children to become more aware of the loveliness of their neighborhood
- To appreciate signs of spring

Materials:

- Jar
- Spices
- Spring flowers

Activity:

Take a walk through the neighborhood (or nearby park) during the springtime. Collect signs of nature that remind us of spring: fresh leaves, grass, flowers, bark. Back in the classroom, let them dry. Then crumble them and place them in a jar. Mix in some spices for a lovely potpourri of springtime. Have the children close their eyes, smell the aroma of the potpourri and talk about what these springtime smells call to mind and how they make the children feel.

Bird Watching In My Neighborhood

Purpose:

- To help children become familiar with bird life in their neighborhood
- To encourage appreciation of other living creatures

Materials:

- Feathers
- Glue
- Construction paper
- Binoculars (optional)
- Music

Activity:

Take the children outside and look for birds. Talk about how they fly, how they look, what they eat, how they communicate; discuss their colors, shapes, sizes, and the parts of their bodies. If possible, use binoculars to get a closer look.

When you return to the classroom, discuss what it might feel like to be a bird. Play some music and encourage the children to pretend to be birds. They might soar, tiptoe, run, peck at food, sing or anything else their imagination dictates.

Then have the children make bird collages by pasting feathers onto paper in a free-form manner, not necessarily in an outline of a bird. This activity will give the children a kinesthetic experience which will help them further relate to what it feels like to be a bird.

Moving To A New House

Purpose:

- To explore feelings associated with the experience of moving to a different home

Materials:

- Empty cartons

Activity:

Moving is often a difficult transition for young children. Since they have not developed a sense of the passage of time, it would be best not to discuss the move until shortly before it will occur; too much advance warning may make the waiting seem endless and unsettling. Here are several activities that can help a child become enthusiastic about the move and help ease the tension he/she may feel about moving to a new house.

- Show pictures of the new area to your child.
- Visit the new house if possible. Meet the neighbors and point out some of the positive aspects of the new neighborhood.
- If possible, take pictures of children in the neighborhood who are your child's age.
- Let your child experience the move by pretending to use cartons to "pack" his/her favorite toys.

Leaving Old Friends

Purpose:

- To help ease the transition involved in moving and leaving familiar friends
- To help children see that friends are kept and not forgotten despite a move

Materials:

- Photographs of friends
- Construction paper
- Stapler
- Envelopes

Activity:

Get photographs of friends from whom the children will be separated after a move. Make a scrapbook by stapling together several sheets of construction paper.

Ask the child to talk about each friend. You might ask about favorite times he/she shared with that friend. Write down what the child says about the friend under his/her picture.

To follow up, write the child's new address on several envelopes and encourage the child to give them out to the friends he/she will be moving away from.

I'm New Here

Purpose:

- To help children explore the feelings associated with a new situation
- To encourage children to be kind to others who are new to the school or neighborhood

Materials:

- None

Activity:

Ask the children if they can think of times they have been in a new place or have started something new. Examples would include:

- a new school
- a new store
- a new home
- going to the hospital
- a new church or synagogue
- going to a new babysitter's house
- a new club or team
- visiting a new doctor or first dental visit

Explore with the children how they felt. Were they excited, scared, lonely, sad, angry, happy, shy, or friendly?

Then encourage the children to discuss how the new situation came to feel more comfortable. Were people kind and friendly to them? Did the "new" feelings go away after a while? Did the place seem more homey after a while? Did they make friends?

Place the children in groups of three. Tell them they will play a pretend game. One of the three children will pretend to be new to the school and the other two children will try to make the "newcomer" feel comfortable. They could show the "new" child around the classroom, introduce him/her to the others, point out the bathroom and where to put his/her coat, talk about the day, etc.

Encourage the "new" child to verbalize feelings associated with being in a new setting and his/her growing feeling of comfort as the "newness" wears off.

The Environment

How Does The Weather Feel?

Purpose:

- To understand weather conditions in a personal, concrete way
- To help guide children in dressing appropriately for various weather conditions

Materials:

- Paper
- Crayons
- Scissors
- Cardboard
- Paper clips

Activity:

Make a "Weather Watcher Doll." Cut out a large figure of a person from cardboard. Tack it to a bulletin board or magnetize it to the refrigerator. Cut out from paper various articles of clothing appropriate to a variety of weather conditions. Some examples might be:

- rain coat
- snowsuit
- umbrella
- hat
- boots
- mittens
- sweater
- bathing suit
- shorts

With the children, check outside conditions for signs of the weather each morning.

Talk about what clothes are appropriate for the "Weather Watcher Doll" that day, and secure these clothes on the doll with paper clips.

This activity will help children learn to dress themselves according to current weather conditions.

Signs of Spring

Purpose:

- To encourage children to feel the beauty and joy of spring, a time of warmth and newness

Materials:

- Colored chalk

Activity:

On a lovely spring day, go outside with the children. Look for and marvel at all the wonderful signs of spring. Note grass, trees, birds, smells, colors, changes in the air, and anything else you or the children may notice.

Invite the children to decorate the sidewalks with colored chalk to express the joy of spring. Explain that the chalk drawings will not stay the way paint does; rather, the rain will make the colors wash away. But that's fine because the group can always go out another time to decorate the sidewalks again.

Seasons

Purpose:

- To encourage the exploration of seasonal changes

Materials:

- A tree in the environment
- Ivory Snow, water, brush, colored construction paper, egg beater
- Fall leaves, crayons, paper
- Sand, shells, paste, cardboard
- Box

Activity:

"Adopt" a tree in the neighborhood. As seasons and weather conditions change the children can look at and touch the tree and discuss changes that are noticeable. Examples are: icicles clinging, buds forming, buds opening, squirrels scampering, leaves drying, changing color, cropping off, hard, cold bark.

During winter, re-create a snowy scene by beating Ivory Snow and a little water with an egg beater. Use the thick frothy mixture to paint designs on brightly colored construction paper. The children create wonderful pictures and the process feels almost like playing with real snow!

For fall, make lovely leaf impression picturees by rubbing a crayon over a sheet of paper on top of a leaf.

For summer, glue, cardboard, and creativity can turn some sand and shells into beautiful collages depicting the textures of a sandy beach.

To challenge the imagination, put items relating to specific seasons into a box. Play a guessing game by having the children name both the item (without looking at it) and the appropriate season. Some ideas might be: a seashell, a mitten, Halloween mask, holiday candle, Christmas card, an acorn, pine cone, beach shovel, suntan lotion, etc.

Morning, Afternoon And Evening

Purpose:

- To help children gain a better grasp of the concept of passage of time
- To help children learn about the sequence of their day

Materials:

- Magazines
- Old greeting cards
- Empty household boxes; e.g. soap suds, cereal boxes, etc.
- Glue
- Stapler

Activity:

Ask children to try to describe what they do on a typical day. After the discussion, emphasize certain things that happen during the morning, afternoon and evening. Have the children make a scrapbook of time: "My Day." Staple 3 sheets of paper together. Label one page "My Morning," the next "My Afternoon" and the next "My Evening." Cut from magazines, greeting cards or household cardboard boxes pictures that depict activities in which the children are involved during the various times of day. Label each one and glue it on the appropriate page. While many activities will be different, children will begin to generalize about activities that occur during the morning, noon and night.

A Big Storm

Purpose:

● To overcome fear of thunder and lightning and downpouring rain

Materials:

● Exciting music

Activity:

During a storm, look outside the window and talk with the children about what you see and hear. Examples might be rain pounding on windows and roofs, trees swaying, wind whistling, lightning flashing, etc. Encourage the children to discuss their feelings as they react to what is happening. As they discuss being scared by the lightning or other natural occurrences outside, you might note,

● "The noise is so loud it hurts my ears."
● "When the sky gets lit up it looks strange."
● "The noise of the thunder comes when we don't expect it, like a jack-in-the-box."

Then stress the positive aspects of the storm, particularly its beauty. You may discuss the interesting designs made by the lightning and patterns formed by puddles or shadows made by trees.

Then put on some exciting, stormy music. Have the children use creative movement to portray some of the natural elements. Examples may include zig-zagging lightning, a bending bush, big, wild droplets of rain, or a leaf being tossed by the wind.

After The Storm

Purpose:

- To further "tame" the wildness of a storm in the experience of the young child

Materials:

- Objects found outside
- Glue
- Cardboard

Activity:

After a rain storm, go outside with the children and explore changes in the environment caused by the storm, such as:

- puddles
- acorns
- streaks on windows
- wet paper
- branches strewn about
- bottle caps
- leaves on the ground
- little stones
- worms
- snails

As you see and touch examples, don't forget to notice smells, such as damp trees, wet earth or soggy leaves.

Collect some of the objects you have found and then glue them on cardboard to make "Rain Collages."

Living Things Grow I: Planting

Purpose:

- To enable children to learn how plants grow
- To encourage children to care about living things

Materials:

- Milk cartons
- Earth
- Grass seeds
- Water
- Paper plates

Activity:

Have the children handle some grass seeds. Note that in order for the seeds to grow, they need earth, water, and sun.

Invite the children to plant the seeds as follows. Cut off the top part of a clean, empty milk carton leaving about six inches. Cut a hole in the bottom for drainage and place on a paper plate. Pack with earth, sprinkle seeds and cover with more earth. Water thoroughly. In a few days you will see shoots of grass peeking up. Be sure to help the children remember to give the plants water when the earth feels dry.

When the grass grows long, give it a haircut with scissors and watch it grow longer again!

Experiment with plant growth by trying to grow some grass under varying conditions.

- Place a container in a dark closet
- Do not water one container
- Keep some seeds in a container without any earth

Children will learn in a concrete way that living things need earth, water and sun to grow.

Living Things Grow II: Growth From Seeds

Purpose:

- To help children learn how plants grow

Materials:

- Fruits with seeds:
  Tangerines
  Oranges
  Grapefruits
  Lemons
  Limes
- Plastic cups
- Paper towels

Activity:

Cut open various fruits with seeds, such as oranges, grapefruits, lemons, limes, tangerines. Invite the children to touch and taste the fruits and pluck out the seeds.

Roll some paper toweling in clear plastic cups. Place some of the fruit seeds between the paper towel and cup and saturate the towel with water. Keep the paper towel wet and watch for beginning signs of growth. Remind the children that these little plants came from fruits they eat.

Living Things Grow III:
To Be A Flower

Purpose:

- To help children use their imagination to "feel" the growth process
- To further understand the life-cycle

Materials:

- Music

Activity:

Discuss the life-cycle of seed growth as experienced in the classroom by planting seeds. Ask the children questions such as:

- "What did the seeds look like?"
- "What did the seeds need to grow?"
- "What happened to the seeds?"

Tell the children they will all pretend to be seeds. Play some music to encourage creative movement. As you pretend to "plant" the seeds, whisper to the children: "First the tiny seeds are sleeping in the warm earth." Then, pretend to sprinkle the "seeds" with water and encourage the "seeds" to grow, grow, grow! Pretend that the sun is out and the "seeds" can dance for joy as they become beautiful "plants."

To help children understand the wonderful cyclical nature of life, tell them: "When the flowers become older, we can take new seeds from them, plant them and then grow new flowers or plants. When the plants get very, very old, they droop and wither. They fade into the ground and become part of the rich earth that feeds new flowers."

Encourage the children to use creative movement to express physically the stages of development.

How Plants Drink

Purpose:

- To help children see how plants drink
- To help children develop a sensitivity toward other living things

Materials:

- Celery
- Water
- Cup
- Red food coloring
- Straws
- Red punch

Activity:

Explain to the children that plants, like us, get thirsty and need to drink. Tell them that they will have a chance to *see* how plants drink. Have each child put some water and red food coloring in a plastic cup. Set a stalk of celery in the liquid. After 24 hours, cut open the celery and examine the red lines formed by the liquid. Talk about how the liquid got there and why.

Invite the children to drink red fruit punch with a straw and pretend to be celery plants drinking liquid.

Tastes From The Garden

Purpose:

- To encourage children to be curious about food in its natural state
- To help children learn how vegetables and fruits grow

Materials:

- None

Activity:

Take a trip with the children to visit a fruit or vegetable garden grown by a parent in the classroom. Talk about the colors, textures, smells and names of the produce. With the permission of the grower, invite the children to carefully pick some of the ripe vegetables. Wash the pieces and then sit together and enjoy tasting the produce in their natural state.

You can also follow this guide for a visit to an apple orchard or a strawberry field, depending upon the season.

Colors In Nature

Purpose:

● To help children learn about and appreciate color in the world of nature around us

Materials:

● Brass fasteners
● Oaktag
● Crayons

Activity:

With the children, make a "color fan". Cut out four pieces of oaktag in small strips.

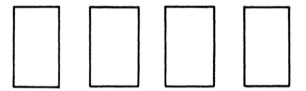

Have the children color one red, one yellow, one blue, and one green. Fasten them all together near the narrow end with a brass fastener.

Talk about each color and tell the children they will take a walk outside to look for things that are the same colors as the ones on their color fans.

Once outside, you can play various matching games. You might say, "First find your red card. Now let's try to find something outside that is red." Or "Can you find something that has two of our colors?"

At a later date, you could add more colors to the color fans and return outside to further explore colors in nature.

Beauty Around Us

Purpose:

• To associate nature with happy, warm feeelings

Materials:

• Large poster board
• Markers

Activity:

Take a walk with the children outside and look for parts of the natural world that make them happy. Encourage them to look up in the sky, out in the distance, down on the ground, and all around them. Let them talk about what they feel when they notice such things as a squirrel running up a tree, a fast-moving cloud, or a burning sun that makes them squint.

When you return to class, have the children sit and talk about what they have experienced. Write their responses on a large poster board. Then let them illustrate this Experience Chart with whichever signs of nature noticed on the walk were their favorites.

Where Did It Come From?

Purpose:

● To help children appreciate order in their environment

Materials:

● Objects from various parts of the classroom

Activity:

Collect an assortment of objects. Place them in a box. Have the children name the objects and put them back in their proper place.

Ask the children, "Why do you think it is important for us to put things back where they came from?" "What would happen if we never knew where anything was?"

It might be fun to do this activity using a timer. Children might see how quickly they could put things back in order.

Where Does My Juice Come From?

Purpose:

- To help children learn about the real sources of the foods they eat

Materials:

- Foods as suggested by the group.

Activity:

In these days of modern conveniences, children rarely come into contact with the real sources of their food products. Hence, it is not unusual for young children to believe orange juice comes from a carton, milk from a bottle, and cookies from a box.

Ask the children to name some foods they enjoy and see if they can tell you where the food comes from. Give the children some firsthand experiences to see, feel, and taste the real food source and preparation. For example, you could squeeze orange juice, make cookies or bread, or cook apples for apple sauce. To further help the children learn about food sources in a direct manner, provide them with appropriate pictures or books, or possibly take trips to such places as:

- a butcher shop
- a bakery
- a farm
- an apple orchard

A Nature Walk

Purpose:

- To encourage children to take a close look at their natural environment
- To help children note change as a lovely, natural occurrence

Materials:

- Magnifying glass
- Large sheet of paper
- Marker

Activity:

Invite the children to take a leisurely walk through their neighborhood to examine objects of nature or things that are part of the earth. Bring magnifying glasses and encourage the children to study closely and describe what they see.

When you return to the classroom, prepare a group language experience chart. Several weeks or months later, reread the story together and then repeat the nature walk. Look for and talk about changes in nature that the group observes and discuss the feelings associated with these changes.

Looking At Clouds

Purpose:

- To help children develop an appreciation of their natural environment
- To encourage an imaginative approach to the exploration of nature

Materials:

- Blue paper
- Glue
- Absorbent cotton

Activity:

Go outside on a fair day. Have the children lie on their backs, look up to the sky and study the clouds. Talk about the clouds' shapes, color, movement, etc. Discuss what the clouds make the children think about or feel.

Go back to the classroom and make cloud collages by gluing cotton to sheets of blue paper in a free-form manner.

Watch The Birds

Purpose:

● To help children develop a nurturing attitude toward birds in their natural habitat

Materials:

● Empty milk carton
● Birdseed
● String
● Scissors
● Foil, wallpaper scraps

Activity:

Go outside with the children and watch for birds. Talk about the needs of wild birds and emphasize how the children can help them by making sure they have food to eat.

In class, make wild bird feeders out of empty milk cartons. Cut holes in the feeder for the birds to reach in. The children can decorate the feeders by stapling aluminum foil or wallpaper scraps to the outside. Place birdseed in the bottom of the feeders and hang them with twine or wire from a nearby tree. As the birds come to eat, talk with the children about how kind it is to care for wild creatures in their natural home.

Through Rose-colored Glasses

Purpose:

• To help children understand that colors can be associated with different feelings

Materials:

• Plastic rings from six-packs of soda or juice
• Colored cellophane

Activity:

Invite the children to make "Magic Glasses" that will make the world appear wildly colored. Cut out double rings from the plastic rings that hold six-packs of juice or soda. Tape colored cellophane across to form "sun glasses". Attach pipe cleaners to either side to form the ear-pieces, being careful to tape the sharp ends.

Encourage the children to try on an assortment of colored glasses. Ask them what they see, and encourage them to talk about how objects look and feel when they are an abnormal color. Invite the children to share feelings they have as they gaze at the world in the rainbow of colors. For instance, you might ask: "How does it feel to see buildings all purple?" or "What does a room that is all red make you think about?"

Sounds Inside and Outside

Purpose:

- To help children tune in to the sounds of their environment and thereby be more in touch with the world around them—the world *inside* the home or school as well as the world *outside*
- To help children develop listening skills by directly experiencing their own immediate world

Materials:

- None

Activity:

Sit very quietly with the children and all close your eyes. Listen very quietly and try to identify all the sounds you hear. Then go outside and try to identify the outdoor sounds you heard. Some examples might be:

- INSIDE
- hum of refrigerator
- furnace
- radiator clanking
- clock
- own breathing
- walls settling

- OUTSIDE
- vehicle passing
- children playing
- birds singing
- horns blaring
- footsteps on pavement
- dog barking

Then encourage the children to talk about how the various sounds make them feel. Some possible experiences might be:

- fire engine: happy
- child crying: sad
- footstep running: excited
- clock ticking: cozy and safe

174

Caring For Animals In Their Natural Environment

Purpose:

- To help children develop a sense of responsibility and nurturing attitude toward animals in their natural environment

Materials:

- Peanut butter
- Pine cones
- Birdseed

Activity:

In the wintertime, discuss with the children the needs of the birds and the difficulties of finding food. Tell the children that they could make feeders that would help the birds find food easily during the cold winter days.

The children can make special bird feeders by taking pine cones, dipping them in peanut butter and then in birdseed. These pine cones can be suspended with twine from a tree outside. If possible, place the feeder within view of a window in the classroom so the children can watch the wild birds enjoy the food that they have provided.

Loving Your Pet

Purpose:

- To encourage children to see a relationship between love and responsibility
- To encourage children to see themselves as caring and loving individuals

Materials:

- Large sheet of oaktag
- Markers or crayons

Activity:

Using a large piece of oaktag, make an experience chart with the children entitled "Ways I Care for My Pet." Ask the children how they show their love for their pets and how they take care of them. Write these suggestions in marker on the oaktag and then have the children illustrate the examples, using additional oaktag if necessary.

Animal Book

Purpose:

- To emphasize the unique characteristics of animals
- To encourage kindness toward animals

Materials:

- Paper
- Crayons
- String
- Two pieces of cardboard

Activity:

Have the children make an animal book. Use two pieces of cardboard for the covers. Punch two holes in each cover and in the paper that will make up the book's pages. Tie the book together with string threaded through the holes.

After going to a park, a zoo, or a walk through the woods, describe some of the animals seen and encourage the children to note their characteristics and activities; eg.,squirrels building nests, gathering their food, etc.

Have the children draw a picture of the animals they've seen in the animal book. The artwork might look like scribbling to an adult, but to a child, it is a very real and satisfying experience. Periodically add new "chapters" to the animal book by repeating this activity. Soon each child will have created a very personal animal book which he/she can enjoy over and over again.

NOTE: If children prefer, cut out animal pictures from magazines and glue them to colored paper in free-form designs.

To Be An Animal

Purpose:

- To expand children's understanding of animals
- To heighten empathy toward other living creatures

Materials:

- Picture books about animals in various settings

Activity:

Talk about the animals the children might see in a particular setting; e.g., a farm, zoo, city street, suburban neighborhood. Read a picture book that deals with such animals. Discuss how the animals look, move, sound, and express their needs. Invite the children to pretend to be these animals. You might step in at times to add new dimensions to the dramatic play, such as by placing a "saddle" on a "pony," or tossing "peanuts" to a hungry "elephant."

This game can be repeated as the children come into contact with more and more animals in varying situations.

Let's Take A Trip

Purpose:

- To ease the children into taking trips so as to make exploring other environments an exciting, nonthreatening experience
- To help children appreciate their world as an ever-enlarging, wonderous place to learn

Materials:

- None

Activity:

This guide is a gradual, building-block approach to taking trips.

In the beginning of the school experience, very young children need to feel secure in their new classroom setting. The new environment will gradually become familiar and the children will then be ready to venture out to other areas in their immediate environment. For example, if the class is in a building with other classes, explore several other floors. If the class is in a single housing unit, visit other areas of the school or its immediately surrounding area.

Short trips that introduce the children to the neighborhood are next in order. To the young child, a simple walk around the block is fascinating. It seems as if he/she has traveled quite a long way.

Once the children feel comfortable in their immediate environment, they will be ready to appreciate further trip experiences such as to the fire station, stores, a zoo, a farm, or any other place in line with your curriculum.

An Airplane Trip

Purpose:

- To explore feelings of excitement and anxiety associated with an impending airplane trip by rehearsing the trip through make-believe

Materials:

- Pictures or storybooks pertaining to air travel
- Seat cushions or classroom chairs

Activity:

Look at magazine pictures, travel brochures, photographs or storybooks that deal with airplane travel. Talk about components of the air travel experience; e.g., buying tickets, checking in, boarding the airplane, buckling seatbelts, taking off, landing and disembarking.

Put chairs or pillows in rows on the floor, placing one or two in front for the pilot(s), and transform the area into an airplane or jet. The children then can pretend to be in the airplane and act out the adventure. Don't forget sounds you might hear, such as engines roaring or landing gear lifting up, or sights you might see out of the window, such as clouds, landing lights, the sun, or houses appearing smaller and smaller. The children might pretend they are on a bumpy ride and move back and forth. Other children might enjoy playing "flight attendant" on the airplane trip.

Living With Others

A major goal in preschool and kindergarten classes is the development of pro-social behavior. This concept might be defined simply as any behavior that benefits another person. Examples of pro-social behavior include sharing, cooperation, and helping, as well as understanding other people's feelings.

Perhaps the most important prerequisite in the development of these behaviors among young children is parental nurturance. Parental affection and caring influences children's moral values and helps to create a positive inclination toward other people.

Research has shown, however, that verbal exhortations or "preaching" to children about sharing, cooperation, etc., do not enhance these behaviors. Rather, children must be provided with opportunities to do things that benefit others. In addition, it has been found that learning to behave positively towards others may elicit such behaviors from others. In other words, children should be given the opportunity to teach one another.

It should be kept in mind that there are several stages in a child's social development. For example, toddler's play is basically egocentric, relating more to things than to people. The next stage of social development is parallel play. During this stage, children play side by side with little or no communication with one another. True social group play is seen when children are genuinely interacting during an activity. At this point, pro-social behavior begins to evolve.

The teacher can manipulate the environment to set up opportunities for pro-social behaviors to develop. It is important always to take into consideration each child's individual needs, however, and to remember that children should be allowed to experience social interaction at their own pace.

Partners Share A Job

Purpose:

- To encourage cooperative actions
- To indicate that jobs get done more easily when people work together as partners

Materials:

- None

Activity:

Ask the children if they can explain what "partners" means and to think of some examples. Some examples could be:

- parents are partners
- parents might have business partners
- we need partners to ride a seesaw
- we usually take partners on class trips

You can help the children elaborate on how these partners work together.

At cleanup time, ask the children to choose partners and work together with their partner on a shared task. Talk about how much easier and faster the job gets done when we share the work!

You Help Me and I Help You

Purpose:

- To encourage children to plan and execute a task with another child
- To encourage children to share

Materials:

- Flour
- Salt
- Water
- Bowl
- Spoon

Activity:

Divide the children into pairs. Give each pair a bowl and a large spoon. Tell the group, "Today we'll make playdough. Each group of two children will work together to make a batch of dough. When you are finished, you may share the playdough."

Recipe For Playdough
1 Cup Flour
1 Cup Salt
1 Cup Water

As much as possible, encourage the children to work out for themselves solutions to problems such as a wobbly bowl or sticky spoon. When necessarey, step in to add suggestions such as, "Why doesn't one of you hold the bowl while the other one stirs (or pours)? Then you could trade jobs."

When the dough is made, emphasize to the children that they really shared the job and worked so well together! Then let the partners play with the dough they have made.

I Like Who You Are

Purpose:

- To help children become aware of how we can express to others our warm feelings for them
- To enjoy the positive feelings of being touched by a friend

Materials:

- None

Activity:

Talk about ways people say, "I like you" without using words. Some examples are:

- rubbing or patting the back
- ruffling the hair
- squeezing shoulders gently
- wrestling in fun
- stroking a cheek
- tweaking an ear

Invite the children to form pairs and encourage them to communicate warmth and affection through some of these and other nonverbal ways.

Some children feel uncomfortable about touching or being touched and that is fine. They should not be forced to play this game. They might prefer to simply talk about the ways their parents or friends show how they like them, or they might pretend to show an imaginary person how much they like him/her.

A Friendship Tree

Purpose:

- To help children further understand what it means to be a friend
- To help children see that friendship grows

Materials:

- Large sheet of paper (butcher paper)
- Paint

Activity:

Ask the children to name a friend. Ask what they enjoy doing with their friends. Talk about various aspects of friendship, including sharing things, having fun times together, getting angry with each other and then making up. Note that just as a tree grows and grows, so, too, does friendship. We feel closer and closer to our friends as we know them longer and do more things with them.

Paint the outline of a tree on a large sheet of paper and invite the children to paint pictures of themselves on this "Friendship Tree."

Listening To Others

Purpose:

● To encourage children to attend to what others say

Materials:

● Tape recorder

Activity:

Sit in a circle with the children and tell them they all will have a chance to make up and tell part of a story. One child begins a story, and each child in turn adds something to the story line. You might help a reticent child by asking pointed questions or gently suggesting a vague idea on which the child could build a story line.

Point out to the group that we must listen to what each person says so we can make the story fun and easy to understand.

If you have a tape recorder or could borrow one, tape the story and play it back at future story-times, again pointing out that this story was possible because all the children paid attention to what the others said.

Learning To Play With Friends

Purpose:

- To foster skills involved in cooperative play
- To further understand the nature of friendship
- To help the child see that he is part of a network of people beyond his family

Materials:

- Paper or material
- Scissors
- Glue

Activity:

Ask the childen to name some of their friends. Talk about what friendship is all about. You might pose some of these questions to add to the discussion:

- "What do you and your friend play?"
- "What do you do to help your friend?"
- "How does your friend help you?"
- "When do you see your friend?"
- "What fun times do you share with your friend?"
- "Do you and your friend sometimes get angry at each other? What do you do about it? Are you still friends, even though you sometimes fight? Why?"

Using material scraps or paper, have the children draw and cut out pictures of their friends and glue them to the paper.

If time permits, let children describe their friends, perhaps emphasizing their friends' favorite characteristics. These stories may be written down as a language experience activity and then put together in a book labeled "Friends."

I Like You

Purpose:

- To help children see that we can like different things in different ways

Materials:

- Construction paper
- Magazines
- Crayons
- Glue
- Scissors

Activity:

Discuss with the children the fact that we can like many different things in many different ways. Encourage the children to finish the sentence "I like_____." They could include people, pets, foods, colors, places, animals, sounds, games, etc.

Then invite them to look through magazines and tear or cut out pictures of things they like. Then have them glue them to construction paper to make a collage called "Things I Like." They could also use crayons on the collage to draw other ideas that come to mind, such as people in their family, pets or even themselves.

Sheet Painting Together

Purpose:

- To see that working together means "cooperating"
- To help children learn how to make space for others
- To feel pride in a group effort
- To encourage sharing

Materials:

- Old sheet
- Water based paint
- Brushes
- Paper plates
- Newspaper

Activity:

Spread plenty of newspaper on the floor. Tape the edges in place. Lay an old sheet on top. Set out brushes and paper plates containing paint.

Let the children sit around the edges of the sheet and paint it together. When it's finished and dry, pin it to a bulletin board or tape it to a wall so everyone can see the result of the group project. Talk about how the children worked together to make this exciting painting.

Trust

Purpose:

- To help children develop a sense of trust in their siblings/friends and in *themselves* as friends

Materials:

- Chairs and tables set up in an open room as a mini-obstacle course.

Activity:

Begin by discussing the concept of "friendship" with children. Possible questions and remarks to guide the discussion are:

- "What is a friend?"
- "Is a friend someone you like a lot?"
- "Friends get angry at each other at times, but they always make up."
- "You trust your friend in a very special way."

Invite the children to play the "Trust Game." Have one child close his eyes. The other child leads the first one around carefully, having him sit on a chair, walk around the sofa, feel the walls, etc. You might introduce this game by saying: "John, close your eyes. Sally will help you go around the room. Sally will be your eyes to see. You know that Sally will not let you hurt yourself. You trust Sally because she is your friend."

After each pair has had a turn, let the partners trade places.

NOTE: This game should be carefully supervised.

I Like You Because Book

Purpose:

- To encourage children to relate positively toward other children

Materials:

- Construction paper

Activity:

Explain to the children that we can all think of something kind to say about each other. Over a period of time, dependent on the size of the group, ask each child to fill in the sentence,

"I like you because _____."

about every other child in the class. Write what the children say on construction paper. Invite each child to draw a picture of the particular child described. Staple together all the drawings and comments which describe a particular child and give the "I Like You Because Book" to the child who is the subject of the book.

You could note to the children that each of us is special in different ways, and these books show us that others think we 're special, too.

A Picnic

Purpose:

- To encourage children to work cooperatively
- To enjoy a group effort that involves the intimate sharing of a meal

Materials:

- Large basket
- Equipment for a picnic

Activity:

Tell the children that you all will be working together to plan and pack a picnic lunch. Discuss and plan the menu together. Be sure to include items such as paper plates, cups, and napkins as well.

Organize the division of labor. Stress that a big meal is so much easier to work out because everyone is working and cooperating together.

Taking Turns

Purpose:

- To help children learn to wait to take turns in order to accomplish a task

Materials:

- Colored yarn
- Clothes pins
- Empty plastic bottle

Activity:

Attach variously colored yarn to clothes pins. Place the clothes pins inside an empty plastic bottle (e.g., a clean, dry bleach bottle) with the strings hanging out. Invite the children to each take one string and pull out the clothes pins. As they all pull at once, a "traffic jam" occurs! The clothes pins cannot all come out at once. Ask, "How can we get our clothes pins out? What would happen if we take turns?" As the children pull the yarn one at a time, their clothes pins come out easily. When the children are finished, point out how easily a job gets done when we wait and take turns.

Parts Of A Whole:
Cooperative Game-Playing

Purpose:

● To offer children an experience in which they must work together to accomplish a goal

Materials:

● Magazine picture
● Cardboard
● Glue
● Scissors

Activity:

Group the children in pairs. Have each pair choose a magazine picture both partners like and glue it onto a piece of cardboard. When dry, cut the picture into an even number of pieces to form a puzzle. Give each child half the pieces.

Tell the children that they worked well together making the puzzle. Now, they can put their pieces together to re-form the picture puzzle. After the children finish the puzzles, say, "What would happen if one of you did not share your pieces? Could the puzzle have been finished?"

Keep the puzzles for future cooperative game-playing.

Connecting: Learning To Work As A Group

Purpose:

- To gently encourage cooperative play

Materials:

- The block area (to include blocks, cars, wooden or rubber people/animals, road signs, etc.)

Activity:

Often several small groups of children build separate structures in the block area. With a few blocks they may connect their structures. They find it thrilling to see their buildings part of a larger whole and themselves part of a larger group effort. "Connecting" works particularly well with children who are not quite ready to engage in cooperative play involving real sharing, taking turns and group planning.

After the connections are in place between block structures, children will learn that small cars can travel the connectors. Then, even though each construction remains unique and intact, the children have begun to engage in group play.

Cooperation Relay

Purpose:

- To encourage children to work together as a unit
- To encourage children to cooperate

Materials:

- None

Activity:

Tell the children that they will have a "Cooperation Relay." Pair the children. In each pair, one child will be a "wheelbarrow" and the other child will be the "pusher." One child holds the other's legs while the other walks on his hands.

Form two teams and have wheelbarrow relay races. Ask what would happen if the "pusher" did not lift up the other child. Would the game work? Explain how the two of them must cooperate to play this game.

Working Together: A Group Hero Sandwich

Purpose:

● To encourage children to work together on a common task and then to enjoy the benefits of the group effort
● To afford an opportunity for children to feel the closeness associated with a shared food experience

Materials:

● Long hero roll
● Assortment of sandwich fillers

Activity:

Slice a long hero or club roll in half lengthwise. Set out an array of sandwich fillers, such as cold cuts, cheeses, lettuce, tomato. Invite the children to work together to fill the roll. When completed, slice off sandwiches for all to enjoy. Point out that everyone is eating a piece of sandwich that all the children helped to create together.

Following Rules

Purpose:

- To help children understand that we have rules to keep us safe
- To cultivate observational and response skills, including coordination of eyes with the rest of the body
- To develop the importance of paying attention

Materials:

These materials are only suggestions; others may be substituted according to their availability.

- Cereal boxes
- Empty cartons
- Inner tube
- Cans
- A balance beam

Activity:

Have a little discussion about rules with your children. You might ask the following questions:

- "Do we have rules in the classroom?"
- "What are they?"
- "Why do we have rules?" (For safety; rules show that people care about us.)

Invite the children to play the Obstacle Course Game. Devise a small course in the classroom, back yard, or playground. It may include the following:

- *cereal boxes* placed far enough apart so the children may step over them easily.

- a *tunnel* to crawl through, made of a large empty carton with both ends open and the tabs tucked in.

- a *balance beam* on which to walk made by carefully placing one long block on two smaller ones at either end.

- a *circle of spaced cans* (with no rough edges) in and around which the children must tiptoe without knocking over the cans.

- an *inner tube* upon which the children must walk without falling off.

Before the children go through the course, they may help you lay it out. You may change the arrangement of obstacles for variety but keep them placed in a large circle.

Say to the children that the obstacle course is a special path. To play the game, they must be sure to follow the *rules*. Let all the childen participate, one by one, while others watch, making sure that each follows the special path. You may choose to make the course more difficult as the children become more skilled in following the rules.

Cooperation

Purpose:

- To learn that a problem may be solved by working together cooperatively
- To experience being different shapes (triangle, square, circle) by using their bodies cooperatively

Materials:

- Flannel board (optional)
- Circle
- Square
- Triangle
- A puzzle with 5 interlocking pieces

Activity:

Ask the children if they know what a picture puzzle is. Show them the puzzle completed. Then give each child a piece and ask them to work *together* to make the puzzle whole again. Tell the childen that when you work together, you *cooperate*.

Ask what would happen if one person would not cooperate. "Would the puzzle be finished?"

Then show the children the paper shapes, one at a time, and ask them if they know the names of these shapes. If they don't, tell them.

Ask the children to lie on the floor and arrange themselves to make each shape. You might ask them how they would go about doing this. If they are having difficulty, you might help place their bodies in the correct positions.

Putting Things Where They Belong

Purpose:

- To help children understand the importance of putting things where they belong
- To foster imagination which could in turn help the children better understand the value of maintaining order

Materials:

- A large carton (to serve as a toy box) to fit 4-5 children *or*
- Separate, smaller cartons to fit one child each
- Records with light, spunky instrumental music

Activity:

Say to the children:

- "Do you ever look for a special toy and can't find it?"
- "Do you ever open a drawer to get some socks but can't because it's SUCH A MESS?!"
- "What is a mess?"
- "Is it easier to find things when they are in the right place?"
- "When things are in the right place, we call it being neat."

Then tell the children we're all going to pretend to be a favorite toy. Ask each child to name and describe a favorite toy. If some children are stumped, you might suggest toys such as: bicycle, puppet, train, truck.

Designate an area as the "toy box" and have the children line up neatly in the "toy box." Then pretend to set each "toy" out. Put on the toy music and encourage the children to pretend to be their toys. They may need some individual demonstrations or questions to help them act out their roles, such as, "Does your bicycle have a bell?" "How does it sound?"

Stop the record and say, "Now playtime is over. All the toys are dropped on the floor into a TERRIBLE MESS."

Let the children fall on the floor in a haphazard fashion. Tell the children, "We're going to clean up this mess! We're going to put the toys back where they belong—in this toy box! When you feel me touch you, come and put yourself away into the toy box."

When all the toys are put away, say, "Now we don't have a terrible mess! We know where the _____ and _____ are! See how it will be easy to find them when we want to play again!"

Sharing

Purpose:

- To help children experience the fun and good feelings associated with sharing
- To help children learn to discriminate textures, colors and names of fruits

Materials:

- 2 of each fruit:
  - Banana
  - Red apple
  - Yellow apple
  - Orange
  - Grapefruit
- Plastic knives
- Mixing spoon
- Plastic spoons
- Small paper plates
- Wash 'n' Dries
- Garbage bags
- Wet sponge
- Table
- Chairs
- Plastic bowl

Activity:

Cup your hands and tell the children you have a make-believe apple. Ask them how they would feel if you ate this make-believe apple *all by yourself?* What should you do? Talk about giving each person a "piece"— sharing your "apple" with everybody—and then pretend to do so and encourage everyone to "eat."

Place the real fruits on the table asking the children what they are. Tell them the names of the fruits if they can't recognize them. Ask the children, "What are *all* these called?" Encourage the children to feel the fruits and talk about their shape, color and feel (soft-hard, rough-smooth).

Ask the children, "How can you *share* your fruit with all of us?" Allow the children to give *you* the solution of making a fruit salad. For instance, if they say, "I could give you a bite," tell them, "That's a way to share, but we might also share a cold, too!" You might ask the children, "How could we each get a little piece of everything? Let's work together, let's cooperate!"

Let the children cut up the fruit in little pieces and put the pieces in the bowl. Each person should get a chance to mix up the salad. As they eat the salad, encourage the children to talk about the different tastes. Can they recognize the fruits in these little pieces?

NOTE: By the way, sometimes it's too hard for some children to share readily. Therefore, keep duplicates of the fruits handy for someone who prefers to keep one fruit and share another!

Birthdays: A Time For Getting And Sharing

Purpose:

- To gain a better understanding of birthdays as being a sign of personal growth and a special opportunity to share with others

Materials:

- Construction paper
- Crayons

Activity:

When a child's birthday occurs, discuss with the children the specialness of the experience. You might note that:

- It occurs only once a year
- Everyone will have a turn to have a birthday
- We celebrate our joy by having a party

Then note that it is true that on birthdays we receive presents and much attention, but birthdays are also for sharing as well. We can make other people happy on our birthdays by making and doing things for or with them.

To encourage this type of celebration in the school, you might incorporate some of the following activities to celebrate a child's birthday:

- All the children could make their own paper hats by decorating construction paper and then stapling it in a cone shape. Perhaps the birthday child may make a crown by cutting a jagged edge along the top and stapling the sides.

- The birthday child and parent could bring in cupcakes baked at home and invite the other children to help ice them.

- Place mats could be made by decorating and fringing construction paper.

- It's fun to hear a special birthday storybook.

As in the case of home birthday parties, it is best to keep the school celebration low-keyed, simple and short. Too much excitement and stimulation can be difficult for the young child to cope with.

This type of party can also be held in the home. Some further hints are:

- Have a small group. A guide to the optimal number of guests to invite is the age of the child plus one.
- Have small favors for all rather than prizes for "winners" of games.
- Time the party carefully. The end of the day is often a cranky period for young children.
- Include some creative sharing experiences, such as group collages or creative movement to music.

Cleanup Can Be Fun

Purpose:

- To help children view this transition time as being fun

Materials:

- None

Activity:

Cleanup time often can be trying for both the teacher and the children. Young childen find it difficult to make transitions from one activity to another, and the hectic atmosphere of cleanup can make them feel even more unsettled and lost. To help young children "change gears" and make cleanup time more fun, try some of the following ideas that treat this period of the day *as an activity* itself, rather than a time to stop having fun and straighten up.

- Set aside certain fun songs to sing while cleaning up. Encourage the children to move to the rhythm as they put toys away.

- Make up a cleanup song with the children and use it every day.

- Play songs from records that have words that encourage the children to straighten, such as "Whistle While You Work," from Disney's "Snow White and the Seven Dwarfs."

- Encourage the children to pretend to be trucks, cars, or trains that carry "cargo" to designated "depots."

- Ask children to find an item of a certain color or beginning with a certain letter to put away.

- On shelves place tape or construction paper shapes to designate the shape of the object that belongs there and pretend the toys are puzzle pieces. This is especially helpful and fun in the block area where the children can match the blocks with their appropriate place by looking for pieces of construction paper cut to the exact size and shape of each type of block.

- Have the children pretend to park the cars in the "garage."

- Invite the children to use cartons to pretend to be shopping; they collect toys and then place them in the proper place. **207**

Each Of Us Is Different

Purpose:

- To develop an appreciation of the uniqueness of each individual

Materials:

- Material for blindfold (e.g., scarf)

Activity:

Discuss with the children that there are many things we all do that are the same. We all eat, sleep, feel happy and feel angry at times. Then talk about how each of us is different and special—and how wonderful it is that that is so.

The following game is a concrete way to help children become aware of the uniqueness of each person: Blindfold one child or, if he/she objects to the blindfold, have him/her close his/her eyes. Have the child try to guess who people are by feeling their faces and bodies. Others' voices may also offer hints. Point out that even though we all have eyes, a nose, mouth, ears, hair, legs, etc., we're all different. There's only one of each of us!

Appreciating Individual Differences I: Animals Are All Different

Purpose:

● To help children see that differences in physical appearance are natural

Materials:

● Magazines
● Scissors
● Large poster board
● Glue

Activity:

Ask the children who have a dog or cat to describe their pets. Note how different each one is in terms of size, color, spots, tails, barks, etc.

Have the childen look through magazines to cut out pictures of dogs and cats. Talk about how they all look different, and note that this is the way it should be. No two animals are exactly alike. That's what makes life interesting!

Make a group collage by gluing these animal pictures to a large sheet of poster board and hang it in the classroom.

Appreciating Individual Differences II: People Are All Different

Purpose:

- To help children see that differences in physical appearance make people interesting and special
- To encourage childen to view differences in appearance in a positive way and to avoid stereotyping others

Materials:

- Magazines
- Scissors
- Large poster board
- Glue

Activity:

Have the children look at the animal collage they made in the previous lesson. Note how the animals look all different; each one is beautiful in its own right. Mention that people, too, are all different and interesting to know, too.

Invite the children to stand in a circle, look around, and note differences among everyone. You might see various sizes, shapes, eye colors, skin colors, hair colors, hair textures, heights, sounds of voices. Note that one is not better than another. Each person is special.

Invite the group to go through magazines and cut out pictures of people of all ages, colors, shapes, sizes, etc. Ask them again to make a group collage and talk about how exciting it is to have so many differences in the world.

I'm Sorry You're Sick

Purpose:

- To develop empathy for a friend who is ill
- To remind ill children at home that friends at school love them, miss them and think about them

Materials:

- Book of wallpaper scraps
- Construction paper

Activity:

When children are sick at home for an extended period, have the class make a gift for the sick child that will remind the child that he/she is missed at school. Fold and staple a sheet of wallpaper like an envelope. The sick child can pin it to the side of the bed for used tissues. The children can also compose a get-well letter in which they communicate their feelings toward their sick friend and send it to the sick child in the envelope.

211

Understanding Children With Special Needs

The integration of handicapped children into the regular school population has been called "mainstreaming." This special section is designed to help children understand the needs of those who might be environmentally, educationally or physically different from others. The emphasis in these activities is that all children are special. Some have needs, however, that require special attention and consideration from the teacher, the children and the school.

213

How Does It Feel Not To See?

Purpose:

- To develop empathy for those with limited or no vision
- To heighten awareness and appreciation of one's own sight

Materials:

- Scarves

Activity:

Discuss with the children how our eyes work for us. You might include in your discussion that:

- eyes help us appreciate the beauty of colors around us.
- eyes can warn of dangers.
- eyes help tell us how other people feel.
- eyes help us have fun; e.g., by allowing us to watch T.V., read, catch a ball.

Explain that some people's eyes do not work well and everything seems dark. Tell the children that you are going to play a game of trying to imagine what it is like not to be able to see.

Using scarves, blindfold several children. If they prefer, they may merely close their eyes. Encourage them to walk around and discuss how they feel and what they experience. You might ask, "Are you scared of bumping into things? Do you know where you are? Can you recognize your friends?"

Ask the children how they might help themselves; e.g., they could use their hands to feel where they are. They could listen carefully to tell who is nearby.

When children take off the blindfolds, have them talk about how it feels to know they really can see.

Seeing With Your Hands

Purpose:

- To help children feel what it's like to have to use your hands to help you see
- To help children appreciate how important vision is

Materials:

- Pen
- Paper

Activity:

Discuss with children how some people cannot see with their eyes. They use their hands as helpers. By feeling little round dots that form kinds of letters, they can read with their fingers! This "dot" language is called Braille.

Make your own "Braille" figures by poking little holes through paper with a pen to form geometric shapes and, on a more advanced level, letters. Have the children close their eyes and trace their fingers over the bumps to "read" the shapes and letters.

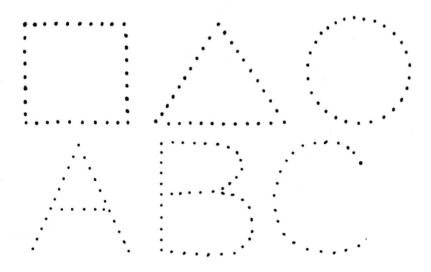

How Does It Feel Not To Hear?

Purpose:

- To develop empathy for those who have limited or no hearing
- To heighten awareness and appreciation of one's own hearing

Materials:

- Ear muffs or ear phones

Activity:

Discuss with the children how our ears work for us. You might include how they help us:

- learn of danger
- enjoy a joke or story
- enjoy music
- hear the telephone
- communicate, or understand what others say

Explain that some people are able to hear just a little, and others can hear nothing at all. Tell the children that they will play a game and imagine what it feels like not to be able to hear.

Place head phones or ear muffs on several children. Encourage the group to act as they usually would: talk, sing, play music, paint, etc. Encourage the children who are imagining the hearing loss to express their feelings. Perhaps they are frustrated, angry, impatient, sad, or lonely. How could they let their needs be known? Then have the children talk about how it feels to know that they really are able to hear.

It's Hard To Walk With A Crutch

Purpose:

- To help children become sensitized to the needs of people who use crutches

Materials:

- Crutches

Activity:

Borrow a pair of crutches from a pediatrician or hospital.

Ask if anyone has had to use crutches, or has anyone seen anybody with crutches? Ask the children if it looks easy. Invite the children to try walking with the crutches. Ask how it feels to get around, sit up and down in a chair, walk in a narrow space, or manage other situations in your environment.

Ask how people who use crutches might feel about having to get around. Discuss ways we could make it easier for them. Some examples are:

- ramps instead of stairs
- wide door openings
- large aisles
- having elevators available

The Mitten Game

Purpose:

- To have children experience what it might feel like to have limited use of their hands
- To develop empathy for others with limited use of their hands

Materials:

- Mittens
- Small objects in the classroom

Activity:

Explain to the children that some people are not able to use their hands well so that simple tasks are very difficult for them.

Tell the children they will play a game in which they will try to imagine what it is like to have trouble using their hands. Place varied objects in the middle of the floor. Have the children put on mittens and try to manipulate these objects. You could include any objects common to the class; however, the following are good suggestions:

- beads to thread
- buttons
- blocks to build with
- puzzles
- books
- crayons and paper
- scissors

Encourage the children to talk about their feelings: annoyance, frustration, impatience, etc.

Have the children remove the mittens and play with the materials. Note how much easier it is to work when they have full use of their hands and fingers.

All About Me

Books

Bemelmans, Ludwig. *Madeline*. New York: The Viking Press, 1939.
Brenner, Barbara. *Bodies*. New York: E.P. Dutton, Inc., 1973.
        Mr. Tall and Mr. Small, Reading, MA: Addison-Wesley Publishing Co., Inc., 1966.
Ellison, V.A. *The Pooh Get Well Book*. New York: E.P. Dutton, Inc., 1973.
Green, Mary McBurney. *Is It Easy? Is It Hard?* Young-Scott, 1960.
        Everybody Eats. Young-Scott, 1950.
Hoban, Russell. *Bedtime for Frances*. New York: Harper and Row, Publishers, Inc., 1960.
Kraus, Robert, *Leo the Late Bloomer*. New York: Windmill Books, Inc., 1971.
Krauss, Ruth. *This Thumbprint*. New York: Harper and Row, Publishers, Inc., 1967.
Lionni, Leo. *Fish is Fish*. New York: Pantheon Books, Inc., 1970.
Mayer, Mercer. *You're the Scaredy-Cat*. New York: Parent's Magazine Press, 1974.
Molarsky, Osmond. *Right Thumb, Left Thumb*. Reading, MA: Addison-Wesley Publishing Co., Inc., 1970.
Ness, Evaline M. *Sam, Bangs and Moonshine*. New York: Holt, Rinehart and Winston, 1969.
O'Neill, Mary. *Hailstones and Halibut Bones: Adventures in Color*. New York: Doubleday and Co., Inc., 1961.
Rey, H.A. and M. *Curious George Goes to the Hospital*. Boston: Houghton-Mifflin Co., 1966.
Sharmat, Marjorie W. *Goodnight, Andrew; Goodnight, Craig*. New York: Harper and Row Publishers, Inc., 1969.
Simon, Mina and Howard. *If You Were An Eel, How Would You Feel?* Chicago: Follett Publishing Co., 1963.
Viorst, Judith. *Alexander and the Terrible, Horrible, No Good, Very Bad Day*. New York: Atheneum, 1973.
        My Mama Says There Aren't any Zombies, Ghosts, Vampires, Creatures, Demons, Monsters, Fiends, Goblins or Things. New York: Atheneum, 1974.
Zolotov, Charlotte. *William's Doll*. New York: Harper and Row Publishers, Inc., 1972.

Games and Materials

Dressing-Undressing Puzzle (Childcraft)
Drink-Wet Dolls (Constructive Playthings)
Flexible Mirror (Creative Playthings)
Health and Personal Care; Picture fold-outs (The Child's World)
Human Body Parts Flannel Aid (Milton-Bradley)
Montessori Self-Help Frames (ETA and ABC School Supply)
My Face and Body (Instructo Flannelboard Aids)

Records

Wake Up Sleepy Eyes Vol. 1, Woody Guthrie (Folkways, 33⅓rpm)
Touch Your Head, *More Singing Fun*, Vol. 2 (Bowmar, 33⅓rpm)

Feelings

Books

Babbitt, Natalie. *The Something*. New York: Farrar, Straus and Giroux, Inc., 1970.
Brown, Margaret Wise. *Goodnight Moon*. New York: Harper and Row, Publishers, Inc., 1947.
Brown, Myra. *Pip Moves Away*. Golden Gate Jr. Books, 1967.
Buckley, Helen. *The Wonderful Little Boy*. New York: Lothrop, Lee and Shepard Books, 1970.
Conta, Marcia and Maureen Reardon. *Feelings Between Brothers and Sisters.* Milwaukee: Raintree Publishers, Inc., 1974.
Flack, Marjorie. *Angus Lost*. New York: Doubleday Co., Inc., 1932.
Hoban, Russel. *A Bargain For Francis*. New York: Harper and Row, Publishers, Inc., 1970.
        Bread and Jam for Francis. Scholastic Book Services, 1969.
Iwasaki, Chihiro. *Staying Home Alone on a Rainy Day*. New York: McGraw-Hill Book Co., 1969.
Kellogg, Steven. *Can I Keep Him?* New York: The Dial Press, 1971.
Klein, Leonore. *Only One Ant*. New York: Hastings House, Publishers, Inc., 1971.
Krauss, Ruth. *A Hole Is To Dig*. New York: Harper and Row, Publishers, Inc., 1952.
Hoffman, Phyllis. *Steffie and Me*. New York: Harper and Row, Publishers, Inc., 1970.
Lobel, Arnold. *Frog and Toad Together*. New York: Harper and Row, Publishers, Inc., 1972.
Mayer, Mercer. *There's a Nightmare in my Closet*. New York: The Dial Press, 1968.
Memling, Carl. *What's in the Dark?* New York: Parents Magazine Press, 1971.
Raskin, Ellen. *Nothing Ever Happens on My Block*. New York: Atheneum, 1971.
Rockwell, Anne. *The Awful Mess*. New York: Parents Magazine Press, 1973.
Simon, Norma. *How Do I Feel?* Chicago: Albert Whitman and Co., 1970.
Udry, Janice May. *What Mary Jo Shared*. Chicago: Albert Whitman and Co., 1966.
Wittels, Harriet and Joan Greisman. *Things I Hate*. Behavioral Publications, 1973.
Zolotow, Charlotte. *The Storm Book*. New York: Harper and Row, Publishers, Inc., 1952.

Games and Materials

Just Imagine: Mini-Poster Cards (Trend Enterprises)
Understanding Our Feelings: 28 Picture Photographs (Constructive Playthings)

Records

"Free to be You and Me" Marlo Thomas et.al. (Bell 1110).
"It's Kiddie Time!" (Topps Li584).
"You'll Sing a Song and I'll Sing a Song" Ella Jenkins (Folkways FC7664).
"Won't You Be My Neighbor" Fred Rogers (Columbia CC34516).
"You are Special" Fred Rogers (Columbia CC24518).

My World Around Me

Books

Balian, Lorna. *Where in the World is Henry?* Scarsdale: Bradbury Press, Inc., 1972.
Brown, Myra. *Benjy's Blanket.* New York: Franklin Watts, Inc., 1962.
Buckley, Heien. *Grandfather and I.* New York: Lothrop, Lee & Shepard Books, 1961.
Carton, Lonnie. *Daddies.* New York: Random House, Inc., 1963.
dePaola, Tommie. *Nana Upstairs, Nana Downstairs.* New York: G.P. Putnam's Sons, 1973.
Eastman, P.D. *Are You My Mother?* New York: Random House, Inc., 1960.
Flack, Marjorie. *Wait for William.* Boston: Houghton Mifflin, Co., 1935.
Krauss, Ruth. *The Backward Day.* New York: Harper and Row, Publishers, Inc., 1950.
Lasker, Joe. *He's My Brother.* Chicago: Albert Whitman and Co., 1974.
Mizumura, Kazue. *If I Were a Mother.* Thomas Y. Crowell, 1968.
Schick, Eleanor. *Peggy's New Brother.* New York: Macmillan, Inc., 1970.
Sonneborn, Ruth. *Seven in a Bed.* New York: The Viking Press, 1968.
                        Friday Night is Papa Night. New York: The Viking Press, 1970.
Steiner, Charlotte. *Ten in a Family.* New York: Alfred A. Knopf, Inc., 1960.
Stover, Joann. *I'm in a Family.* New York: David McKay Co., Inc., 1966.
Yashima, Taro. *Umbrella.* New York: The Viking Press, 1958.

Games and Materials

Family Tree Mobile Material for three generations on each side of the family (Creative Playthings).
Judy Playtrays: Clothing, Food, and Currency Sets (ABC School Supply)
Judy Storyboard: Building A House
Puzzle: Rubber fit-in figures of family (Creative Playthings)

Records

"A Place of Our Own," Mister Rogers (Pickwick International Inc., 33⅓rpm)
"My Street Begins at My House," Ella Jenkins (Folkways, 33⅓rpm)
"Sounds Around Us," ("Around the House")(Scott Foresman, 7 inch 33⅓rpm)
"The Sleepy Family" (YPR; 78rpm)

The Community

Books

Brown, Margaret Wise. *The Little Firemen.* Young-Scott, 1952.
Freeman, Don. *Inspector Peckit.* New York: The Viking Press, 1972.
Gergaly, Tibor. *Busy Day, Busy People.* New York: Random House, Inc., 1973.
Lenski, Lois. *Policeman Small.* Henry Z. Walck,1962.
Merriam, Eve and Ronni Solbert. *Mommies At Work.* New York: Alfred H. Knopf, Inc., 1961.
    Boys and Girls, Girls and Boys. New York: Holt, Rinehart and Winston, 1972.
Scarry, Richard. *What Do People Do All Day?* New York: Random House, Inc., 1968.

Games and Materials

Community Puppets (Childcraft)
Home and Community Puzzles (Playskool)
Instructo Activity Kit: Community Helpers at Work, 4 helpers, 40 pcs.
Our Helpers Play People (Milton Bradley)
People in the Neighborhood: Safety/Health Helpers (The Child's World)
Playskool Puzzles: Community workers, 6 in set, 14-19 pcs. each
Tools and Trades: Set of 4, 10 pcs. in each puzzle (Childcraft)
Trip to the Zoo: A scenic floor puzzle with four sections, 36 pcs. (Childcraft)

Records

"Building a City" (YPR, 33⅓rpm)
"Men Who Come to My House"/"Let's Be Firemen"/"Let's Be Policemen" Young People's Record (YPR, 33⅓ rpm)
"Won't You Be My Neighbor?" Mister Rogers (PII) Pickwick International Inc.

The Environment

Books

Brown, Margaret. *The Dead Bird.* Reading, MA: Addison-Wesley Publishing Co., Inc., 1958.
Carrick, Donald. *The Tree.* New York: Macmillan, Inc., 1971.
Duvoisin, Roger, *The House of Four Seasons.* New York: Lothrop, Lee & Shepard Books, 1969.
Fisher, Aileen. *I Like Weather.* Thomas Y. Crowell, 1963.
Hoff, Syd. *When Will It Snow?* New York: Harper and Row Publishers, Inc., 1971.
Keats, Ezra Jack. *The Snowy Day.* New York: The Viking Press, 1962.
Krauss, Ruth. *The Happy Day.* New York: Harper and Row Publishers, Inc., 1949.
     The Growing Story. New York: Harper and Row Publishers, Inc., 1947.
Kuskin, Karla. *The Bear Who Saw The Spring.* New York: Harper and Row Publishers, Inc., 1961.
Lenski, Lois. *Spring Is Here.* Henry Z. Walck, 1945.
     Now It's Fall. Henry Z. Walck, 1948.
     I Like Winter. Henry Z. Walck, 1950.
Sendak, Maurice. *Chicken Soup With Rice.* Scholastic Books, 1970.
Tresselt, Alvin. *I Say the Sea Come In.* New York: Lothrop, Lee & Shepard Books, 1965.
Udry, Janice. *A Tree is Nice.* New York: Harper and Row Publishers, Inc., 1956.

Games and Materials

Four Seasons: 4 piece puzzle for each season (Childcraft)
Seasons (Milton Bradley)
Seasons (Instructo Activity Kits)
We Dress For Weather (Instructo)

Records

"A Springtime Walk" Lucille Wood Picture Song Book (Bowmar, 33⅓rpm)
"Another Rainy Day Record" (Bowmar, 33⅓rpm)
"My Playmate the Wind" (YPR, 78 and 45 rpm)
"Raindrops Keep Falling On My Head," B.J. Thomas, any recording

Living With Others

Books

Alexander, Martha. *Nobody Asked Me if I Wanted a Baby Sister.* New York: The Dial Press, 1971.
Anglund, Joan. *A Friend is Someone Who Likes You.* New York: Harcourt Brace Jovanovich, Inc., 1958.
Arnstein, Helene. *Billy and Our New Baby.* Behavioral Publications, 1973.
Beim, Jerrold. *The Smallest Boy in the Class.* New York: William Morrow and Co., Inc., 1949.
Berger, Terry. *A Friend Can Help.* Milwaukee: Raintree Publishers, Inc., 1974.
Beskow, Elsa. *Pelle's New Suit.* New York: Harper and Row, Publishers, Inc., 1929.
Brenner, Barbara. *Nicky's Sister.* New York: Alfred A. Knopf, Inc., 1966.
Brown, Myra. *Best Friends.* Chicago: Childrens Press, 1967.
Cohen, Miriam. *Best Friends.* New York: Macmillan, Inc., 1971.
        Will I Have a Friend? New York: Macmillan, Inc., 1967.
Fassler, Joan. *The Boy with a Problem.* Behavioral Publications, 1971.
Hoban, Russell, *A Bargain for Francis.* New York: Harper and Row, Publishers, Inc., 1970.
Jarrell, Mary. *The Knee-Baby.* New York: Farrar, Straus and Giroux, Inc., 1973.
Keats, Ezra Jack. *Peter's Chair.* New York: Harper and Row Publishers, Inc., 1967.
Krasilovsky, Phyllis. *The Shy Little Girl.* Boston: Houghton Mifflin Co., Inc., 1970.
        Susan Sometimes. New York: Macmillan Inc., 1962.
Lasker, Joe. *He's My Brother.* Chicago: Albert Whitman and Co., 1974.
Lionni, Leo. *Frederick.* New York: Pantheon Books, Inc., 1967.
        Swimmy. New York: Pantheon Books, Inc., 1963.
Marshall, James. *George and Martha Encore.* Boston: Houghton Mifflin Co., 1973.
Scott, Ann. *On Mother's Lap.* New York: McGraw-Hill, Inc., 1972.
Sharmat, Marjorie. *Gladys Told Me to Meet Her Here.* New York: Harper and Row, Publishers, Inc., 1970.
Vigna, Judith. *Gregory's Stitches.* Chicago: Albert Whitman and Co., 1974.
Viorst, Judith. *I'll Fix Anthony.* New York: Harper and Row Publishers, Inc., 1969.
Waber, Bernard. *Ira Sleeps Over.* Boston: Houghton Mifflin, Co., 1972.
Watson, Jane Robert Switzer, and J. Hirschberg. *Sometimes I'm Jealous.* Golden Press, 1972.
Zolotow, Charlotte. *My Friend John.* New York: Harper and Row, Publishers, Inc., 1968.
        The Quarrelling Book. New York: Harper and Row, Publishers, Inc., 1963.
        A Tiger Called Thomas. New York: Lothrop, Lee & Shepard Books, 1963.

Records

"It Could Be a Wonderful World" (Motivation Records MR10)

Printed in the United States
1388600002B/66